WHAT'S CHURCH ALL ABOUT?

And Other Tricky Questions about the Church

JOHN HONNER

A GUIDE FOR TEACHERS, CATECHISTS, AND PARENTS

Paulist Press
New York / Mahwah, NJ

Cover image by Jorge Anastacio / Shutterstock.com
Cover and book design by Lynn Else

Library of Congress Cataloging-in-Publication Data
Names: Honner, John, author.
Title: What's church all about? : and other tricky questions about the church : a guide for teachers, catechists, and parents / John Honner.
Description: New York / Mahwah : Paulist Press, [2022] | Summary: "This sequel to Does God Like Being God? and Did Jesus Have a Girlfriend? aims to help parents, teachers, and catechists answer the tricky questions that young people ask about Church"— Provided by publisher.
Identifiers: LCCN 2022012642 (print) | LCCN 2022012643 (ebook) | ISBN 9780809156306 (paperback) | ISBN 9780809187935 (ebook)
Subjects: LCSH: Church—Miscellanea. | Catholic Church—Doctrines—Miscellanea.
Classification: LCC BX1746 .H57 2022 (print) | LCC BX1746 (ebook) | DDC 262/.02—dc23/eng/20220808
LC record available at https://lccn.loc.gov/2022012642
LC ebook record available at https://lccn.loc.gov/2022012643

ISBN 978-0-8091-5630-6 (paperback)
ISBN 978-0-8091-8793-5 (e-book)

Published by Paulist Press
997 Macarthur Boulevard
Mahwah, New Jersey 07430
www.paulistpress.com

Printed and bound in the
United States of America

For Bonnie and Nick
and their domestic church:
Georgia and Daniel, Clementine and Adam, Yvonne and Benedict,
and Daisy, Mary, Lucy, Jemima, Alfred, and Annaliese,
with much gratitude and great hope.

CONTENTS

Acknowledgments...vii

Introduction: Gathering the Pilgrim People of God ix

PART ONE: QUESTIONS ABOUT THE CHURCH 1

1. Church? What's that all about?.. 3

2. Doesn't religion do more harm than good? 6

3. Why do you still go to Church?... 10

4. How did the Church last so long? 13

5. Is it all right for me to go to the Godspel Church?................ 16

6. Why is the Church so hung up on sex? 20

7. Why is the Church against same-sex marriages?................... 24

8. Why can't women be priests?... 29

9. Why can't priests be married? 33

10. How can I know my vocation? 38

11. Why do you need that tall hat?....................................... 41

12. Why do we have to go to Church? It's so boring!................. 44

13. Why can't the Mass always be like that?.......................... 48

14. Why does the Church oppose abortion and euthanasia? 50

15. Do they all have superpowers? 54

16. If God forgives everyone, why does hell exist? 57

17. Will my dog go to heaven? 61

CONTENTS

PART TWO: ADVANCED TOPICS **67**

18. Why is tonight different from all other nights? A domestic Church.... 69

19. Cathedrals and Caravans: A Synodal Church.. 73

20. Marian and Petrine: A Holy and Apostolic Church................................... 76

Conclusion: Where to from here? A Church for the Future 79

ACKNOWLEDGMENTS

If it takes a village to raise a child, it takes a caravan to raise a Christian. After a lifelong journey, many thanks are well overdue. I owe almost everything to my companions from the Society of Jesus and my friends in the Uniting, Anglican, and Baptist Churches associated with what is now the Australian University of Divinity.

In more recent years, I have been privileged to work with MacKillop Family Services, Jesuit Social Services, Edmund Rice Community Services, and several Catholic Social Services, as well as the Pastoral Planning Committee of the Catholic Diocese of Wollongong, the CatholicLIFE office of the Archdiocese of Canberra and Goulburn, the major superiors of the Society of Mary, the Australian Sisters of Charity, the Trustees of Mary Aikenhead Ministries, the Daughters of Charity, the Trustees of St. John of God Health Care, the National Council of the St Vincent de Paul Society, the Council of Edmund Rice Education Australia, the Australian Association of Ministerial Public Juridic Persons, the Ministerial Leadership Program of the Australian Catholic University, students from the Australian Institute for Theological Education, and, almost as if born out of time, a preparatory writing group for the 2021 Plenary Council of the Catholic Church in Australia. I thank all the good and wonderful people associated with these ministries for their faith, service, intelligence, humor, humility, hope, and company. I also thank members of the Catholic parishes of Yarraville, Nowra-Berry, and Pittwater, who have been my fellow travelers in the day-to-day journey of faith. The Spirit manifested among all these women and men has much influenced my reflections on the Church.

Outside of Church circles, and perhaps saving me from living in a clerical bubble, I am most grateful for being welcomed into the operations of both the Victorian Centre for Excellence in Child and Family Welfare and the Victorian Council of Social Service. I learned not only how little I knew about organization, vision, and commitment, but also that there are great numbers of people in civil society who seek to build a better human community through care and service.

I also acknowledge the contributions of the teachers and youth workers who have fed questions into this series of books. I particularly thank Peter Bierer, the coordinator of the Catholic Office for Youth and Young Adults in the Archdiocese of Adelaide, for his insights into the concerns of young Catholics and his steadfast work; nonetheless, he should not be held accountable for all the answers offered here.

I owe much to my family too—my carefully chosen parents and my sister and brothers—for their constant love and support, even when I may have been acting a little strangely. I thank my wonderful nieces and nephews in all their variety, along with their numerous spirited children. Several of the stories included here have come from these families and are used with their permission—though names and details have been changed to protect the innocent.

I also acknowledge the expertise and encouragement of the staff at Paulist Press. I particularly thank Paul McMahon, the editorial director at Paulist Press, for his care and support.

Last but far from least, I thank my wife, Colleen, for her love and her unfailing belief in the importance of these small books, and all my extended family, in all their variety—my own communion of saints.

INTRODUCTION

GATHERING THE PILGRIM PEOPLE OF GOD

Young people dream dreams. They want a better Church than the one they see today. Following the 2018 Synod of Bishops on Young People, Pope Francis begged members of the Church to listen to the young, to be open to change, and to be "attentive to the signs of the times":

> A Church always on the defensive...which leaves no room for questions, loses her youth and turns into a museum....How, then, will she be able to respond to the dreams of young people? Even if she possesses the truth of the Gospel, this does not mean that she has completely understood it; rather, she is called to keep growing in her grasp of that inexhaustible treasure. (*Christus Vivit* 39, 41)[1]

The Greek word in Scripture that we translate as "Church" is *ekklesia*, which literally means "the called-out ones." In the New Testament, *ekklesia* means something like "the gathering of the community" or "the assembly." All the followers of Jesus were included. The *ekklesia* grew out of a community centered on Jesus.

The Church exists to make Jesus visible in the world and to continue the mission of Jesus. In this sense, the "Church" includes all Christians of all denominations. The Church is not a static, abstract ideal. It is neither a building nor a multinational corporation. It is a living and breathing gathering of people inspired by Jesus. It is a gathering on the go, a caravan, the pilgrim people of God.[2]

Formal membership of the Church comes through baptism. The Catholic Church recognizes every Christian baptism as valid, provided the baptism is with water and

---

1.   Pope Francis, *Christus Vivit: Christ is Alive*, Post-Synodal Apostolic Exhortation (March 25, 2019). See also the various contributions of Massimo Faggioli, beginning with his *Pope Francis: Tradition in Transition* (Mahwah, NJ: Paulist Press, 2015).

2.   The Second Vatican Council of the Roman Catholic Church describes the Church as a pilgrim Church, and its members as pilgrims and the people of God. See, e.g., *Lumen Gentium: Light for the Nations*, The Dogmatic Constitution on the Church (November 21, 1964), nos. 7, 21, 48, 50.

uses the Gospel formula, "I baptize you in the name of the Father, and of the Son, and of the Holy Spirit" (see Matt 28:19). In this respect, the Catholic Church includes all Christians. And so it should. The word *catholic* means "universal" or "including all."

The Church has a human history, starting with communities of Christians in places like Jerusalem, Antioch, Ephesus, Corinth, Alexandria, and Rome. In their first two centuries of existence, they came to agree on common Gospels, a common baptism, and a common Creed. Thus a "whole" Church, a "universal" Church, took shape. That's why it is called "Catholic."

The Church has frequently been challenged to grow and change over its two thousand years. There have been times of persecution, prosperity, pain, and renewal. Sometimes, the Church has split into different denominations; other times, it has gotten stuck in the past. Even during the last century, there have been many prophetic calls for the Church to renew itself. The great Dominican theologian Yves Congar, reflecting on the decline in faith in Europe after the First World War, wrote, "It seemed to me that this was due to the fact that the Church was showing to the world a face that betrayed, rather than expressed, its true nature in accordance with the Gospel and its own profound tradition."[3] He later had a major influence on the Second Vatican Council, which ran from 1962 to 1965 and which described its chief purpose as "to inquire how we ought to renew ourselves, so that we may be found increasingly faithful to the Gospel of Christ."[4]

Today, more than half a century after Vatican II and despite many reforms to governance, teaching, and liturgy, the renewal of the Church remains a pressing matter. It is a wintry season for Catholics in many parts of the world. Some are hanging onto their faith by their fingernails. Others dream of a Church that shows the face of God; a Church that walks with Jesus; a Church that is welcoming and inclusive; a Church that is for the poor; a Church that is authentic; a Church where people are filled with love, freedom, hope, and joy; a Church where people feel they can belong; and a Church that is thereby holy.[5] This renewal is yet to be achieved.

I am not meaning to be bleak or pessimistic. After fifty years of service in various ministries in and around the Church, I know the goodness of its members and the self-giving love they show day after day in a rich array of ministries. Nonetheless, it

---

3. As quoted in Yves Congar, *My Journal of the Council* (Adelaide: ATF, 2012), vi. This diary gives an extraordinary insider's view of the workings of the hierarchical Church, sometimes inspiring, sometimes self-serving. It could only be published after his death!

4. "Message to Humanity" issued at the beginning of the Second Vatican Council (October 20, 1962).

5. This was the shared vision for the Church discerned by a preliminary writing group in preparation for the 2021 Plenary Council of Australia.

is delusional either to think that the Church should just go on as it did in the past or, even more unwisely, should return to what it was thought to be in the so-called glorious days of the 1950s. Most young people find the Church far too staid. We need to be "attentive to the signs of the times." We are being drawn into a new future. We need to recognize the signs of the Holy Spirit at work. We should include young people. We need to hear their questions.

~ ☺ ~

Today, the Church is flourishing in the East and the South of our planet. In the dollar-rich secular nations, however, where Christendom was once universal, the Church is declining in numbers and spirit. Truthfully, most young people in these wealthy nations—and this includes many young Catholics—don't bother much about Church today. They might care about spirituality, about justice, about the environment, and about the poor. They might have a sense of the divine and an admiration for Jesus. Yet, for whatever reasons—usually a combination of social pressure and the Church's lack of credibility and relevance—young people are not asking questions about the Church except, predictably, "Why do I have to go?"

One American sociologist, Christian Smith, found that "the situation regarding Catholic youth and the church is indeed very grim."[6] Others are more optimistic, noting that young American Catholics "are more religious than many older people realize, but, compared to their pre–Vatican II grandparents, they are more likely to be Catholic on their own terms."[7] The general trends are incontrovertible. A 2021 Gallup poll reveals that whereas 66 percent of people in the United States born before 1946 claim church membership, only 50 percent of Generation X and 36 percent of millennials identify as members of a church.[8]

Christian Smith, in the wake of his comprehensive survey of *Young Catholic America*, makes a telling observation:

> If there's one thing I know about younger people, whether they are 13 or 28, nearly every last one of them thinks of Christianity as a set of rules and regulations, do's and don'ts. They aren't necessarily fighting against

---

6. Christian Smith, *National Catholic Reporter* (June 13, 2015). Smith is Professor of Sociology and Director of the Center for the Study of Religion and Society at the University of Notre Dame. He was lead author of *Young Catholic America* and related studies.

7. William D'Antonio, *National Catholic Reporter* (December 6, 2014). D'Antonio taught at Notre Dame and was later Professor of Sociology at the University of Connecticut. He was lead author of *American Catholics in Transition* and related studies.

8. See Jeffery M. Jones, "U.S. Church Membership Falls below Majority for First Time," Gallup, March 29, 2021, https://news.gallup.com/poll/341963/church-membership-falls-below-majority-first-time.aspx.

that. That's simply what they think Christianity is—a set of moralisms. The church is a place of moralistic requirements....What many think about "religion" is: It's just not something that matters to them. Religion is seen as something they might take an interest in later in life, like life insurance. They aren't angry about it. It's just given a presupposed dismissal.[9]

While there are some young people deeply committed to their Catholic faith, particularly where their parents bear a strong witness, Smith found that the vast majority of young Catholics in America have drifted away from the Church.

A recent survey of European young adults, commissioned as part of the preparations for the Synod on Young People, shows that religious adherence and religious practice vary considerably across cultures. Many young people profess no religion, and few of those who do profess religion regularly attend religious services. In countries where there still exists a close connection between religion and government, there is greater religious affiliation. For example:

> The proportion of young adults [aged 16–29] with no religious affiliation... is as high as 91% in the Czech Republic, 80% in Estonia, and 75% in Sweden. These compare to only 1% in Israel, 17% in Poland, and 25% in Lithuania. In the UK and France, the proportions [with no religious affiliation] are 70% and 64% respectively....
>
> Only 2% of Catholic young adults in Belgium, 3% in Hungary and Austria, 5% in Lithuania, and 6% in Germany say they attend Mass weekly.... Weekly Mass attendance is 7% among French, and 17% among British, Catholic young adults.[10]

There is a temptation to blame our contemporary culture for this decline in religious observance. Secularism, materialism, individualism, and consumerism may be symptoms rather than causes, though the connections between liberalism, individualism, and private property are surely factors. The causes of decline may also rest with a Church that, despite many beacons of hope, seems to have gotten stuck in its European past. Even committed young Catholics report experiencing close-minded

---

9. "Souls in Transition: An Interview with Christian Smith," *Yale Reflections* (2014), https://reflections.yale.edu/article/seeking-light-new-generation/young-souls-transition-interview-christian-smith. See also Christian Smith et al., *Young Catholic America* (Oxford: Oxford University Press, 2014).

10. Stephen Bullivant, *Europe's Young Adults and Religion* (London: Benedict XVI Centre for Religion and Society, 2018), 3.

attitudes and feeling ignored.[11] As one participant at the Synod on Young People put it, "Sadly, many people my age see the Church as a weighty institution disconnected from reality, yet her mission is to give us Jesus, who is the way, the truth, and the life."[12]

No wonder that Pope Francis calls for a renewal of the Church and a return to "the freshness of the beginning"[13] in order that "the Church's customs, ways of doing things, times and schedules, language and structures can be suitably channeled for the evangelization of today's world rather than for her self-preservation" (*Evangelii Gaudium* 27).[14]

~ ◯ ~

This book is intended to contribute to getting back to the freshness of the beginning. It is a sequel to *Does God Like Being God?* and *Did Jesus Have a Girlfriend?*[15] The project was prompted by the questions young people asked and the pleas of teachers for a practical theological guide. The first book in the series, reflecting on young people's tricky questions about God, was relatively easy to write, because young people are interested in God and there are many wonderful things they dream about God. The second book, on questions about Jesus, turned out to be a joyful task, because young people like Jesus as a person, and they ask many intriguing questions about him. Furthermore, the four Gospels provide a relatively modest set of resources for exploring these questions.

Responding to young people's tricky questions about the Church, however, has proven to be a much more challenging task. There are many issues, many different opinions, many writings about the Church, as well as a good deal of smoke and mirrors. Many of the questions arise from a relatively narrow and negative experience of Church. As a result, there are no specific questions here about some of the usual *Catechism* topics, like the seven sacraments, purgatory, infallibility, or the beatific vision. Many of the questions, nonetheless, lead to an exploration of key statements

---

11. See, e.g., Trudy Dantis and Stephen Reid, *Called to Fullness of Life and Love: National Report on the Australian Catholic Bishops' Youth Survey 2017* (Canberra: Australian Catholic Bishops Conference, 2018), 34–37, https://www.mn.catholic.org.au/media/3679/acbc-youth-survey-report-sm.pdf.

12. Emilie Callan, "Looking Back at the Synod," Salt + Light Media, January 21, 2019, https://slmedia.org/blog/looking-back-at-the-synod-most-frequently-asked-questions.

13. Pope Francis, Address to Italian Bishops, May 23, 2013.

14. Pope Francis, *Evangelii Gaudium: The Joy of the Gospel* (November 24, 2013).

15. John Honner, *Does God Like Being God? And Other Tricky Questions about God* (Mahwah, NJ: Paulist Press, 2019); and John Honner, *Did Jesus Have a Girlfriend? And Other Tricky Questions about Jesus* (Mahwah, NJ: Paulist Press, 2022).

in the Apostles' Creed about "the holy Catholic Church, the communion of saints, the forgiveness of sins, the resurrection of the body, and life everlasting."

For older people who believe that the Church is meant to be a flourishing and triumphant institution, the decline of religious practice among the young can be rather depressing. Hopefully, this book offers some enlightenment, encouragement, and consolation. Perhaps the Church has its seasons, perhaps sometimes it is a poor Church, a remnant, a small seed that seems to die but then grows into a great tree.

Pope Francis certainly exhibits great hope in young people. In his post-synodal exhortation, he applauds the "audacity of youth" and encourages us to "invest" in the "fearlessness" of youth. He asks them to "be courageous," to "say the truth," and to ask "the raw questions."[16]

The answers given in this book to young people's raw and fearless questions will not solve all the Church's current problems. They do not constitute a comprehensive theology of the Church, but they may offer direction and hope. They are intended to provide parents, teachers, and ministers with stories and ideas that will expand their sense of Church and suggest words and images that might better engage their children and students. While we must always respond to the *person* asking the question before we go about answering their *question*, fresh thinking may also help.

I will not repeat here material from the introductory chapters to the first two books in this series, except to note that they explored the wonder of God, the life and mission of Jesus Christ, the simplicity of theological method, the importance of the Bible, the reasonableness of faith, and the conditions for the development of Church teaching. Some readers may find my regular references to Scripture, to Catholic teaching, to recent pontiffs, and particularly to the *Catechism of the Catholic Church* rather narrow and backward-looking. But Scripture is our guide to living the faith, and the *Catechism* provides a valuable summary of Church teaching across the centuries. These help us get to the heart of the issues—the "freshness of the beginning"— and the radical DNA in the roots of Christian faith. Some may find my reading of Church teaching one-sided, and to a degree that is true, because I am on the side of the young and the excluded. Nonetheless, the reflections here remain well within the intentions of the Gospels and the bounds of orthodoxy.

I have also drawn on the contributions of the great twentieth-century theologians of the Church, both Catholic and Protestant—particularly Henri de Lubac, Yves Congar, Karl Barth, Dietrich Bonhoeffer, and Karl Rahner—and twenty-first-century

---

16. Pope Francis, *Christus Vivit*, no. 233, and "Opening Address" at meeting prior to the Synod of Bishops on Young People, October 5, 2018, nos. 10, 178.

theologians like Phyllis Zagano on the role of women in the Church, and the former Anglican Archbishop of Canterbury, Rowan Williams, on the unity of the Church and the Church's relationship to the world. Massimo Faggioli's thought-provoking reflections on the history and existential reality of the Church have also had an impact. My final chapters also draw attention to the writings of younger Catholic women theologians. For those looking for even fresher thinking, I have continued to address some questions in light of contemporary sociology and science. Some footnotes are included to provide either evidence or guidance for those who seek further information. As with the earlier books, you can begin at any chapter that interests you, and then work your way through other parts of the book. I hope that these reflections are, therefore, both orthodox and engaging.

This book has two parts. The major part reflects on the tricky questions that children and young people ask about the Church. The second and shorter part, called "Advanced Topics," is more for adults. It reflects on some of the central concerns of the Church and what it might become. While this series of books was originally intended to help teachers and parents in talking with young people about Christian faith, feedback suggests that these reflections have been appreciated by many adults, even the venerable, and all who are forever young at heart.

The influence of Pope Francis is obvious in this book. He is a living symbol of the Church's ability to change. With him, I hope that "once the Church sets aside narrow preconceptions and listens carefully to the young...it allows young people to make their own contribution to the community, helping it to appreciate new sensitivities and to consider new questions" (*Christus Vivit* 65). And I hope that a young person called Junior—you will meet him in the first chapter—might be included in such a listening. He has much to tell us.

Part One

QUESTIONS ABOUT THE CHURCH

1

CHURCH?
WHAT'S THAT ALL ABOUT?

Church is about the important things in life: creation, birth, meaning, belonging, love, truth, forgiveness, healing, spirit, dying, and hope in the future. It was Junior who asked the question, "Church? What's that all about?" It happened like this. It was Junior's birthday weekend. He was turning thirteen. As part of an annual ritual, Junior flew into town on the Friday with his dad and his younger brother, Dogboy. They were on pilgrimage. They went to the beach, did some eating and shopping, and then swam in their hotel's rooftop pool. Dogboy had Junior's smartphone in the pocket of his swimmers when he jumped in. It was at the deep end. That didn't work out well. After an exercise in forgiveness, the three of them went out for souvlaki and pizza with a favorite uncle and aunt.

On Saturday afternoon, they would attend their football team's first home game of the season. They would wear team gear, stand in line for sausage rolls and meat pies, sit in rows on hard seats, and roar with the crowd. They would listen to Dad's stories about his first visit to the ground as a boy with his own father, which happened shortly after the dinosaurs became extinct. They would be instructed about the legends of the game as they limped past like living martyrs. The traditions of the club and the laws of the game would be repeated. They were being inducted into a place of heritage, a place where they could belong. This was their gathering.

The final stage of this annual ritual was a visit to Dad's father, who happens to be known as Papa.[1] On Sunday, however, they had to fly back home earlier than usual because one of the boys, who shall remain nameless, hadn't finished a school assignment due on Monday morning. Junior had the job of phoning Papa to arrange a visit on their way to the airport on Sunday morning. Papa's reply was unexpected.

---

1. Though not to be confused with Papa Francisco, as Pope Francis is known in the world Church.

"I'm sorry," he said, "but I'm going to Church on Sunday morning." Junior was almost speechless. Much taken aback, he said to Dad, "Church? What's that all about?"

You may be one of those good people who find any code of football boring and can't see the point of it, but many young men love it. They love the drama, the risk, the action, the courage, the commitment, the team spirit. However, many young men find Church boring and can't see the point of it. There's something to consider here. Junior knew what Church was, or at least he thought he did, but he had not experienced the drama of the liturgy, the risk of faith, or the cost of discipleship. What had discombobulated him, then, was why his not very religious grandfather would want to go to Church rather than see his grandsons.

Junior's bewilderment was understandable. He had been to a parish primary school and now attended a Catholic high school. Religion came with the uniforms, but it had not yet entered his soul. Going to Church, as for most young people, was not an attractive proposition. There are more demands than rewards and it takes a lot of effort to go. The people wear weird clothes, tell boring stories, sit on hard seats, sing uncool songs, talk about their heroes, and queue up for nourishment. It is very like going to football in these respects, but the football team and their followers feel like they mean it.

Junior has also probably been affected by his peers and their influencers. Even if the world of football is manipulated by broadcasters with an interest in profits from gambling and alcohol, and even if football might be part of the globalization of superficiality,[2] it is cool. It does something to meet the desire we all have for belonging and enchantment. Indeed, for Dad, his team's home ground is holy ground, so much so that he'd like to get his ashes scattered there.

~ ◯ ~

When Junior asked his question—"Church? What's that all about?"—his dad didn't reply with a theological dissertation. He said something like this, "Well, Papa is getting older you know, and I think it's become important for him to get his priorities in life right." This was an authentic answer. Junior didn't say anything at the time. He is still trying to find out what is important in life.

It was Arrigo Sacchi, perhaps Italy's greatest football coach, who said that "football is the most important of the least important things in life." The Church, however, is about the most important of the important things in life: creation, birth,

---

2. This phrase may have come from the former Superior General of the Jesuits, Father Adolfo Nicolas, better known as "Nico."

meaning, belonging, love, truth, forgiveness, healing, spirit, dying, and hope in the future. While there are many definitions of *Church*, in essence it is a community of people who share the goodness of Jesus in their day-to-day care for each other and for all creation, from before birth to beyond death.[3] That's what Church is about, and that's why it was so important for Papa.

---

3. The *Catechism* says much the same, though in more complicated language: "The word 'Church' means 'convocation.' It designates the assembly of those whom God's Word 'convokes,' i.e., gathers together to form the People of God, and who themselves, nourished with the Body of Christ, become the Body of Christ." *Catechism of the Catholic Church*, §777.

2

DOESN'T RELIGION DO MORE HARM THAN GOOD?

This question prompts two immediate responses. First, we should note that while religion includes faith, in some respects it differs from faith. Religion is what happens when people try to organize faith. This can sometimes lead to the abuse of faith and can indeed do harm. Religion can sometimes lose touch with the heart of faith. It can get in the way of God's dealings with us. Jesus clearly thought that religion did much harm. He was scathing of some of the religious leaders of his own day. For example, he is reported as saying to the Pharisees and the teachers of the law, "You abandon the commandment of God and hold to human tradition" (Mark 7:6–8). Or again, "Woe to you, scribes and Pharisees, hypocrites! For you lock people out of the kingdom of heaven" (Matt 23:13).

Second, and more seriously, it should be acknowledged that harm has been done in the name of religion, even if sometimes unintentionally. Furthermore, religions can be inherently harmful if they infantilize believers and prevent them from growing into a deeper adult faith.

A more discursive response needs to unpack what lies behind these issues. Young people hear terrible reports about religions. They hear about the sexual abuse of children, corrupt finances, and hypocrisy in teaching and practice. They also hear about the excesses of the Crusades, the Church's opposition to science, its collaboration in the colonization of the so-called New World, its mistreatment of First Nation peoples, and horrific religious persecutions. They hear about Islamist terrorism, crazy religious cults, and religious fanatics. The frequency of these reports and the concentration of bad news can come from the way the algorithms behind social media channel stories, but there is nonetheless a kernel of truth behind most of them.

These negative reports have had a cumulative effect. International surveys show that around half the people in the wealthiest countries in the world think religion does more harm than good.[1] Dozens of recent books argue for and against the case. The facts are clear: there is widespread suspicion of religion among younger generations in the developed world. This does not mean that younger generations lack spirituality or a quest for meaning. It means that what they hear about religions does not attract them.

While it is arguable that religion has done harm, it is equally arguable that religion has done good and can continue to do good.[2] Christianity, for example, has produced wonderful human beings like Dorothy Day and Martin Luther King Jr. or Francis of Assisi and Mother Teresa of Calcutta. They may not have been perfect, but they dared to travel into the heart of their faith. Christianity also developed beneficial institutions like hospitals, schools, and universities. Some say it created the conditions for the rise of science. Furthermore, Christians continue to contribute to social movements today. For example, two Quakers, Dorothy and Irving Stowe, were among the founders of Greenpeace, and Peter Benenson, a Catholic of Jewish descent, created Amnesty International. We could go on, but perhaps we would appear defensive rather than listening.

The choice for young people is either to give up religion or to go deeper into the heart of religion. Young people are more likely to have minds that are open rather than closed. They want to have an intelligent conversation about religion in its current context. My conversations usually go like this:

Young Person: Religion does more harm than good.

Me: I can't argue with that.

YP: You mean you agree?

Me: Not quite. I mean that I can't argue with an opinion. I can understand why people might think that religion does more harm than good, but it's a sweeping

---

1. For details of a 2017 Ipsos global survey, see https://www.ipsos.com/sites/default/files/ct/news/documents/2017-10/GlobalAdvisor-Religion-2017.pdf. See similar results from surveys conducted in the *Huffington Post* (2014) and *The Guardian* (2006).

2. A notable critic of religion is Phil Zuckerman, *Society Without God: What the Least Religious Nations Can Tell Us about Contentment*, 2nd ed. (New York: New York University Press, 2020). Notable defenders of religion are Keith Ward, *Is Religion Dangerous?* (Grand Rapids, MI: Eerdmans, 2006); and John Dickson, *Bullies and Saints: An Honest Look at the Good and Evil of Christian History* (Grand Rapids, MI: Zondervan, 2021).

statement. It's like saying governments do more harm than good, or teenagers do more harm than good. You can't prove or disprove sweeping statements.

YP: Is that a sweeping statement?

Me: Ha. You have to say what you mean by religion. I think it's different from faith. Religion is what you get when you organize faith. And to prove this statement about religions doing more harm than good you would have to explore all religions across the centuries and measure every incident of harm and good and then weigh them against each other. That's impossible.

YP: But a lot of people say it's true.

Me: Not all widely held views are true. It was once widely held that the sun rose and set, and that children should be seen and not heard, and that a woman's place was in the home. Are they true?

YP: But the Church is on the nose. Wouldn't you agree with that?

Me: Absolutely. But that's a horse of a different color.

YP: Whaaat?

Me: I mean, that's a slightly different argument. You were saying religion did more harm than good. We can talk about the Church if you like. Or do you want to talk about faith in Jesus doing more harm than good? Jesus is all right, isn't he? Even Jesus was critical of religious leaders in his own time.

YP: Sure. He cares about the lost sheep. But the Church isn't all right. It pretends to be holier than thou, and it clearly isn't.

Me: Yes, sadly, if by Church you mean the organized institution....

YP (being kind): It's not that there aren't a lot of good people like you that I admire, but the optics are terrible.

Me: Optics?

YP: What it looks like.

Me: Ah.

And so the discussion continues. We have listened, we stay friends. We can now say that "religion" is different from "faith" and we can agree that Jesus is all right.

On another day, I might note that science has found that having religious belief does more good than not having religious belief in terms of mental health and life outcomes. A recent survey conducted by the Mayo Clinic concludes that "religious involvement and spirituality are associated with better health outcomes, including greater longevity, coping skills, and health-related quality of life (even during terminal illness) and less anxiety, depression, and suicide."[3] Similarly, the Mental Health Foundation in the United Kingdom found that "religion plays a central role in the processes of reconstructing a sense of self and recovery."[4]

    3. Paul S. Mueller, David J. Plevak, and Teresa A. Rummans, "Religious Involvement, Spirituality, and Medicine: Implications for Clinicals," *Mayo Clinic Proceedings* 76 (2001): 1225.

    4. Deborah Cornah, *The Impact of Spirituality on Mental Health* (London: Mental Health Foundation, 2006), 2.

3

WHY DO YOU STILL GO TO CHURCH?

I used to say that I went to Church because it reminded me that I was not the center of the universe. It gave me a chance, I would say, to open myself up to the holy mystery at the heart of the world. When we get too self-centered, we can make our little selves the center of the immense universe, but when we seek the face of God, we slowly come to recognize a loving mystery at the heart of creation. While going to Sunday Mass might take little more than an hour in the rhythm of my week, it is also a moment in eternity for me—a celebration of my destiny in God's infinite love.

Ironically, during the COVID-19 pandemic, I haven't physically gone to Church at all. Thanks to the internet, I have been able to watch Masses from around the world, eventually settling in the Diocese of Lismore in Australia and finding much consolation in the way its Carmelite bishop presides at the liturgy and opens up the Bible readings. While not able to receive communion physically, I can still find a deep sense of being in the company of Jesus.

The Mass is not meant to be a private pleasure, nor a spectacle watched from a distance. The Eucharist is a shared meal, a force for unity, a call to service, and a communion with both my neighbor and my Creator. Soon, we will return to our local parish Mass. The liturgy may not be as inspiring and consoling, but this is the real world, the world that God enters and embraces. I like the people I have come to know in my local Church because they seek holiness in life too. They opt for hope and meaning. We are fellow travelers. I love the actual Church that I am part of, despite its ordinariness and its failings. A neighbor recently asked me where I went to Church. I said that I was "a clinging-on Catholic." She smiled. I think she understood.

I realize that I now go to Church because I love the Church. I love it because it is part of a much bigger picture. I am not talking about greatness in numbers or power, but greatness in heritage and promise. As Dorothy Day once observed, love sees the deep good in things. Love sees beyond faults. Love sees to the heart.

I could go to a different kind of Church—one that is more vibrant and more welcoming, more humble, more honest, more successful, or one that came closer to my taste in music. In the end, though, nobody gets the kind of Church they would design for themselves. This is because the Church is full of other people. It is God's Church. Rowan Williams says that "believing in the Church is really believing in the unique gift of the other that God has given you to live with."[1] This doesn't mean I should be complacent about the shortcomings of my Church, but it does mean that I should rejoice at difference, even when it does not entirely suit me.

I also go to Church because it is part of my Sabbath. Keeping the Sabbath is surely the least demanding of the Ten Commandments. I love the quiet. Nobody is going to phone me, ask me to help them, talk about politics, or complain about the shortage of persimmons in the supermarket. I can be at peace. The rituals—blessing myself with holy water, genuflecting, making the Sign of the Cross, going down on my knees, receiving communion—are spiritual and physical exercises that enhance my life. Furthermore, as much as possible I avoid undertaking burdensome work on a Sunday. We may go for a walk by the beach, sit on the balcony in the evening. We enjoy the Sabbath. We give thanks.

There are some Church buildings, whether grand or humble, that are holy places. They feel like they have been prayed in, they feel as if God is present. The Irish have special words for these locations. They call them *thin* places. "Heaven and earth are only three feet apart," as the Irish saying goes, "but, in the thin places, that distance is even shorter." Most of our churches and cathedrals are too cluttered or too self-congratulatory to be thin spaces, whereas the holy churches and chapels are mainly pure empty space. There is room for the infinite.[2] Dorothy Day said of the Cathedral in San Francisco,

> St. Mary's Cathedral is a window to the infinite, lifting the human spirit to the infinite and eternal beauty which is God....Here is a place of transcendent beauty, and it is as accessible to the homeless in the Tenderloin as it is to the mayor of San Francisco. The Cathedral in San Francisco is one of the few places where the poor can go and sit down and be with God in beauty.[3]

---

1. Rowan Williams, *Tokens of Trust: An Introduction to Christian Belief* (Louisville, KY: Westminster John Knox Press, 2007), 106.

2. I thank Bishop Greg Homeming, OCD, of the Diocese of Lismore for this insight, and for several other reflections that have found their way into this book.

3. Anne Stricherz, "The Absolutely Amazing Catholic Conversion Story of Dorothy Day," Cora Evans blog, accessed May 13, 2022, https://www.coraevans.com/blog/article/The-Absolutely-Amazing-Catholic-Conversion-Story-Of-Dorothy-Day.

Being in a Church needs to feel like being on a mountaintop, or on a small boat in the middle of the sea, or under the stars, or on the open road. You will find Jesus in those places too.

We can find or construct holy places for ourselves. God deals with each of us individually, meets each of us in a unique way. Jesus used to go into the hills to pray, but village synagogues were also on his itinerary. He threw the merchants out of the temple in Jerusalem because the house of God should be a house of prayer. And the time is coming, he told the Samaritan woman, when true worshipers will be neither in the mountains nor in the temple, but in spirit and truth (see John 4:21–23). Ultimately, though, it is what is in our hearts that makes a place holy, our sense of the abiding presence of God.

If young people are to find God in our church buildings, they need to be inspiring spaces for a new future. They may be venerable, but they should not be museums of superficial tastes. They need to be able to include all the pilgrim people of God in their rich variety. Only holy people should be allowed to build holy places. They may need help from good architects and great artists—think of the breathtaking chapels designed by Matisse or Le Corbusier, or Chagall's church windows—and, yes, they may need help from young people.

4

HOW DID THE CHURCH LAST SO LONG?

The person who asked me this unexpected question is without guile. I wasn't quite sure why he asked it. He may have been wondering how the Church has lasted for so long, given that it has been so scandal prone. Or possibly he was thinking more deeply about what it was that could have sustained the Church for two thousand years while most other powerful institutions have passed away. What is the secret of the Church's longevity? This question is ultimately about the essence of the Church.

The Church started as a scattered and persecuted religious minority from the Middle East. It grew into European Christendom and then into a world church. According to Vatican figures, at the end of 2019, 48 percent of the world's Catholics were living in South and North America, followed by 21 percent in Europe, 19 percent in Africa, 11 percent in Asia, and just 1 percent in Oceania. I quite like being part of the 1 percent.

Some may regret that the Catholic Church is no longer the triumphant partner of the Holy Roman Empire. This is a misleading triumph, however, because during the Middle Ages, when the Church was dominant in Europe and had a presence around the Mediterranean Sea, it was virtually unknown in sub-Saharan Africa, the far East, the Americas, and Oceania. Today, by contrast, the Catholic Church may have lost its dominance in one continent, but it has become a global Church. It has a presence in virtually every culture and society, and it continues to grow.[1] Furthermore, because Christianity is manifest not only in the Catholic Church but also in many other Christian communities seeking to follow the way of Christ, there is greater growth to consider. The future of the Catholic Church is surely connected with the future of the whole of Christendom.

---

1. According to Vatican figures, in 2019 the worldwide Catholic population exceeded 1.34 billion, which continued to be about 17.7 percent of the world's population. It marked an increase of 16 million Catholics, which was a 1.12 percent increase compared to 2018, while the world's population grew by 1.08 percent.

A marketing analysis might explore the Church's survival in terms of luck, the excellence of the brand, the quality of the people and culture, the continuing demand of customers, or its ability to adapt to new circumstances. Even though the Church may seem monolithic and inflexible, its history shows that it keeps growing. It may avoid trends and fashions, but it is not stuck in a particular time and place. Some may think that holding onto Tradition means continuing to do things exactly the way they were done in the past, with the same rules, the same uniforms, the same rituals, and so on. This, however, may be nostalgia rather than Tradition. Tradition continues to unfold through the story of the power of the Holy Spirit working among us. Tradition is not for preserving the past so much as it is for finding the future.

What, then, is the essence of the Church? Think about this. The Nicene Creed has four parts: first, belief in God, the Creator; second, belief in Jesus as both divine and human; third, belief in the Holy Spirit as the Lord and giver of life; and fourth, and seemingly on a quite different level, belief in "one, holy, catholic, and apostolic Church." The Church is thus given a high place in Christian faith, as if an extension of the Trinity, and that's what it is. The Church is primarily intended to reveal the light of Christ to all the world rather than to hold onto that light only for itself. Perhaps that is why it has lasted so long.

Another key theological point is that Christian faith is not a belief in a particular Church—neither the Coptic Church, nor the Orthodox Church, nor the Maronite Church, nor the Anglican, Lutheran, Baptist, Episcopalian, Methodist, Presbyterian, Uniting, Pentecostal, or Evangelical Churches, nor even the Roman Church—but belief in a one, holy, catholic, and apostolic Church, as stated in the Nicene Creed. This is a Church that proceeds from a God of incomprehensible love. In other words, the Nicene Creed—and the Apostles' Creed for that matter—reminds us that the Church flows from God's mission. The Church doesn't have a mission so much as being God's mission.[2]

The Church is thus essentially the sign of God's ultimate act of love for the world. It is where God is at work, which is everywhere. What it communicates is more important than how large or powerful it is. As Karl Rahner, one of the great theologians of the twentieth century, noted, "The Church is everywhere: in the last resort its nature and its function remain independent of its numerical relationship

---

2. See Steven Bevans, "The Mission Has a Church: Perspectives of a Roman Catholic Theologian," conference paper (Edinburgh: 2010), http://edinburgh2010.org/en/resources/papersdocuments8ad4.pdf?no_cache=1&cid=34423&did=22380& sechash=43e9d7d6, and similar articles.

to the total world-population."[3] The secret to how the Church has lasted so long, then, is not to be found in the rise or fall of its numbers. It is to be found in God's presence and promise. So how has the Church lasted so long? Because God's love endures forever.

Church may have many manifestations and expressions, and some of these will be flawed, skewed, and self-important, but it will also continue to renew itself, as it has done so often in the past. But now comes the deeper question. Do we know what the Church of the future will look like? Will it continue to be centered in Rome? How will it continue to renew itself? Will it flourish? Will there be more vocations to religious life and the priesthood? The answer to these questions is rather blunt: we do not know! In the big picture, these things ultimately do not matter.

Perhaps the Church is meant to be a great haul of fish. Or perhaps it is a light on a stand or a small seed that falls on good ground. I doubt it is meant to be a triumphant multinational power. Jesus's kingdom is not of that kind. Perhaps it is meant to be a poor church for the poor, a scattered remnant, a diaspora. Whatever the case, this Church will continue in history, holy and flawed, always seeking renewal. What matters is that God's love endures forever.

There are some who say they believe in Jesus but not in the Church. Perhaps they mean they don't believe in the institutional Church. Believing in Jesus, however, always entails believing in his mission and hence believing in the community that continues his mission. Belief in God's love is the basis for belief in the Church, and God's love is the reason why the Church has lasted so long.

---

3.   Karl Rahner, "The Future of the Church and the Church of the Future," in *Concern for the Church: Theological Investigations XX*, trans. Edward Quinn (New York: Crossroad, 1981), 105.

5

IS IT ALL RIGHT FOR ME TO GO TO THE GODSPEL CHURCH?

This is different. Here is a young Catholic who actually wants to go to church, and who even seeks permission to go to church, but is it the right church? The Godspel Church is a made-up name, in order to protect privacy, but it could be one of many contemporary Christian churches like Hillsong, the Salt Church, the C3 Church, or the late lamented House of the Gentle Bunyip. These churches attract young people with outstanding contemporary religious music. Its members strive to make newcomers welcome. It seeks to be Christ centered and Bible based. Young people are engaged, given a sense of belonging, and helped to grow as disciples of Jesus.

To any young person asking a question like this, I would say, first, how wonderful it is that he or she is feeling called to grow in their faith. I might note that a good test of the authenticity of a Church is whether its members condemn other Christian communities as diabolical heretics or respect them as fellow travelers, because being very critical of other Christians is rarely a sign of the Holy Spirit. I would add, as St. Ignatius of Loyola teaches in his *Spiritual Exercises*, that God deals with each one of us in a unique way, and your interest in the Godspel Church might be God's way of calling you into a deeper relationship, particularly in this growing stage of your life. I would then try to explain, as St. Ignatius learned, that for a person trying to lead a good life, the signs of God's calling are gentle, subtle, and persistent. So, if this thought of going to Godspel persists, and if you feel a deep, lingering consolation, then this might be God's calling. However, according to St. Ignatius, if you happen to have felt an intense excitement that passes quickly and leaves you feeling a little empty, then this might not be God's calling. Having done all that, I could also point out how the Catholic Church teaches that "many elements of sanctification and of truth are found outside the visible confines of the Catholic Church" (*Catechism* §819).

This advice is a reformulation of the Church's teaching on acting in accord with our conscience. Quoting the Second Vatican Council, the *Catechism* declares that conscience is "present at the heart of the person....There he [or she] is alone with God, whose voice echoes in his [or her] depths." And, further, "A human being must always obey the certain judgment of his [or her] conscience" (§§1776, 1777, 1800). As things turned out, the young person asking this question listened to Godspel music for a time but decided not to go to the Godspel Church. This was a step in a continuing journey of faith.

~ ◯ ~

But why are there so many Churches? This is the scandal of disunity. Only sixty years ago, there was considerable and scandalous animosity between various Christian churches. When I was a young boy at a Catholic school, I was given the impression that there was only one true Church and, lucky for me, that true Church happened to be the one I was in. Outside that Church, we were told, there was no salvation. However, being in the only Catholic family on the street, I also heard hurtful comments from other boys and girls. When I was around seven or eight, a little girl called Sandra yelled at me when I was walking home from school, "You can't be Australians; you are Catholic; you worship the pope." Sandra and I had been misled, in different ways, by the grown-ups in our lives.

The Second Vatican Council asserted that salvation comes from Christ rather than from the Church, and that the Catholic Church is a broad Church. Those who seek God with a sincere heart, it declared, "may achieve eternal salvation."[1] There is only one Church, the Church of all time, the Church of Jesus Christ, the Church of the apostles.[2] Godspel, Hillsong, Salt Church, C3 Church, and the Gentle Bunyip are all part of it. We have moved beyond antagonism between churches to friendship. The next step is communion.

There have always been divisions and differences in the Church, perhaps even among Jesus's own disciples. For example, according to Matthew's Gospel, Jesus's mission had originally been only for "the lost sheep of the house of Israel" (Matt 10:6), but then ended up being a mission to "make disciples of all nations" (Matt 28:19). The Acts of the Apostles are full of robust discussions as to whether non-Jews should be included in the Christian community, particularly if they refused to be circumcised.

---

1. See Second Vatican Council, *Lumen Gentium: Light for the Nations*, nos. 14, 16; and *Catechism of the Catholic Church*, §§846, 847.

2. See Henri de Lubac, *More Paradoxes* (San Francisco: Ignatius Press, 2002), 25. See also Second Vatican Council, *Lumen Gentium*, no. 8.

The leaders of the various parties then met in a council in Jerusalem. After much had been said, Peter spoke. He was for tolerance and inclusion, not intolerance and exclusion, and he declared that God "has made no distinction between them and us" (Acts 15:9).

While disunity is a scandal, differences of vision can lead to the renewal of the Church. Sometimes, they have gotten tied up with nationalism and politics and have been of global significance, like the schism between the Eastern Orthodox Churches and the Roman Catholic Church in the eleventh century, or the Reformation in the sixteenth century. Sometimes, they have been acting in accord with their consciences and what they perceive to be the unchristian teachings or practices of incumbent authorities, as happened with the healthy disruptions caused by dissenting and non-conformist churches in Great Britain—Baptists, Congregationalists, Quakers, Methodists, and Wee Free Presbyterians. They were all trying to be true to the gospel.

Roman Catholics, believing themselves to be part of the oldest and most original Church, going back to St. Peter and the apostles, sometimes claim uniqueness by an appeal to their history. This is not quite accurate, given that the oldest continuing churches are to be found in places like Damascus in the Middle East. What Roman Catholics can appeal to, however, is the long-standing tradition, going back to Jesus's own words and the Acts of the Apostles, that we should be one, that the Church should seek unity, and that there is a place for a successor of Peter as the first among equals.

At the Second Vatican Council, the Catholic Church formally confessed its own failings in the lead-up to the schisms and divisions of the past. It now recognized members of other Christian denominations "with respect and affection as brothers and sisters."[3] Francis takes this recognition a step further. He does not speak of "our separated brothers and sisters," which has a hint of estrangement, but rather of all Christians being pilgrims journeying alongside one another. This means that "we must have sincere trust in our fellow pilgrims, putting aside all suspicion or mistrust and turning our gaze to what we are all seeking: the radiant peace of God's face."[4]

Newly emerging churches are often born out of an enthusiastic group's love of Jesus, a dissatisfaction with the established churches, and a desire to get back to the freshness of the beginning. The Bible quite rightly is their chosen compass. More complicated, though, is their intention to make the Bible their sole authority, particularly if only a fundamentalist reading is allowed. Decisions about what texts went into the

---

3. Second Vatican Council, Decree on Ecumenism, *Unitatis Redintegratio*, November 21, 1964, nos. 3, 7.
4. Pope Francis, address to Brazil's national council of Christian Churches, February 18, 2021.

Bible and how we are to interpret them today are decisions made by the community of believers under the guidance of the Holy Spirit.[5]

If the Church is the community of the baptized that makes Christ visible, then Godspel and many other small new churches are freshly constructed parts of it. Many young Catholics enjoy Godspel music, as with my own parish youth group. Some say they can feel the Spirit in the Godspel Church, and they learn something new about the Bible, but they continue to find Jesus in the sacrament of the Eucharist. We need all three: good music, good preaching, and a shared Eucharist! Thank God that we have moved beyond antagonism between churches to friendship. The next step is communion.

---

5.   For further reflections on the preeminence of the Bible and how to read Scripture, see "Why is the Bible important?" in John Honner, *Does God Like Being God?* (Mahwah, NJ: Paulist Press, 2019), 9–12.

6

WHY IS THE CHURCH SO HUNG UP ON SEX?

This is a major concern that young people have about the Church. Following the 2018 Synod on Young People, and quoting from pre-synod papers, Pope Francis acknowledged that, for young people today, "sexual morality often tends to be a source of 'incomprehension and alienation from the Church, inasmuch as she is viewed as a place of judgment and condemnation'" (*Christus Vivit* 81). Surveys of young people and young adults show that the Church's attitude toward sexuality along with the dreadful sexual abuse perpetrated by its ministers are two major reasons for their disengagement from the Church.[1]

The wording of this question suggests that the Church has an excessive interest in sex, and more than it does on pressing issues like the growing divide between the rich and the poor or the destruction of the environment. Furthermore, the words *hung up on* imply that this excessive interest is unbalanced.

An answer to this question could start with two points. First, because sex is about flesh, love, and life, and because Jesus was about becoming flesh, self-giving love, and the fullness of life, the Church should be expected to have much to say about sex. Sex is profoundly part of human life. Second, it might be gently noted that many young people in contemporary western societies also appear to be much interested in sex, if pop culture, sexting, and rates of access to pornography are any indication. So, while the Church seems to be so often saying no to sex, many young people seem to be heading in the opposite direction, asking, "Why not?"

The Church does not mean to be saying, "Stop having a good time." It means to be saying, "Start having a good time." Much here hinges on what is meant by "good."

---

1. For example, the Australian Catholic Bishops Pastoral Research Office report, *Catholics Who Have Stopped Attending Mass*, found that 31 percent of Catholic parents of children attending Catholic schools gave "disagreement with the Church's teaching on, or attitude to, personal sexual issues" as the reason why they do not go to Mass (Canberra: ACBC, 2007), 5. Christian Smith found young American Catholics to be "discarding Church teachings on sex, birth control, abortion, etc." See Christian Smith et al., *Young Catholic America* (Oxford: Oxford University Press, 2014).

The Church draws on Scripture, on its Tradition, and on a branch of philosophy called ethics, which is intended to help us make right and good choices. Ethicists help us to live happier lives. Ethical treatises might be seen as sophisticated "self-help" books. Ethics, on the one hand, inevitably demonstrates that the right and good thing to do is more than a matter of personal opinion. On the other hand, if rigorously applied in the abstract, ethics can turn into rules of the road rather than wisdom for life. For example, a focus on physical actions, as if persons were just material objects, can oversimplify complicated human realities. This is one reason why the Church's teaching can seem unbalanced. It has not helped young people, either, when this teaching is imposed by old celibate males who seemed unable to deal with clerical child sexual abuse.[2]

Another reason for the Church's teaching on sex seeming unbalanced is that, for many periods of the Church's history, a dualist view of human nature has prevailed. A dualist view sees the soul and body as separable entities, like a driver in a motor car, and where the soul is good and the body is bad, where spirit is pure and flesh is corrupt, where heaven is holy and the world is sinful, and where virginity is for saints and marriage is for the desperate. Sex was not seen as something beautiful, tender, self-giving and loving, something created by God, something sacramental. Married couples, as a result, were never candidates for sanctity. It is astonishing that the Catholic Church's first canonization of a wife and husband as saints together— St. Marie-Azélie Martin and St. Louis Martin—only occurred in 2015.[3]

Despite its abiding influence, dualism is contrary to Christian belief. The world and the flesh may be transient, but they are not inherently evil. As we read in Genesis, God made the world, and it was good. And in Jesus, "because God has taken on flesh," all flesh can "disclose the glory of God."[4] The human person has both material and spiritual characteristics but is always a single entity. Love is as profound and complex as the human person.

The Catholic Church has long held with a natural law ethics, which is based on the idea of an essential unchanging human nature and on human reason, which is an essential part of human nature. The *Catechism* declares that "the natural law is

---

2. The French Independent Commission on Sexual Abuse in the Church recommended that the Church "closely examine how the paradoxical obsession of Catholic morality on issues of sexuality could be counterproductive in the fight against sex abuse." See "Sexual Violence in the Catholic Church in France 1950–2020: Summary of the Final Report," October 5, 2021, 21, http://www.themediareport.com/wp-content/uploads/2021/10/2021-France-abuse-report.pdf.

3. And that was surely because they were the parents of a virgin and a nun, St. Thérèse of Lisieux, who had been canonized in 1925.

4. Dorothy A. Lee, *Flesh and Glory* (New York: Crossroad, 2002), 39.

nothing other than the light of understanding placed in us by God" and hence "is universal in its precepts and its authority extends to all." It follows that we should shape our ethical decisions in accord with what it means to be human. There is nonetheless a significant caveat about the natural law. On the one hand, "the natural law is *immutable* and permanent throughout the variations of history" because it is based on God-made essential human nature, which does not change with time or place. On the other hand, because places, times, and circumstances change, "application of the natural law varies greatly" (*Catechism* §§1955, 1956, 1958, 1957).

In the light of Christian faith, to be human is to be in the image of God, both as an individual person and as a member of a community of love. In recent years, particularly through the influence of personalist philosophies of John Paul II, the Church has paid more attention to the personal and sacramental dimensions of sex. Francis, after the Synod on Marriage, made a further important acknowledgment: "In no way, then, can we consider the erotic dimension of love simply as a permissible evil or a burden to be tolerated for the good of the family. Rather, it must be seen as gift from God that enriches the relationship of the spouses" (*Amoris Laetitia* 152). Sex, then, should not be reduced to commerce, entertainment, or self-indulgence. It is much more profound than that.

Young Catholics might be surprised to know that when a couple gets married in the Church, the minister of the sacrament of marriage is not the priest. The priest is just the witness representing the community. *The couple themselves are the ministers of the sacrament.* Furthermore, *the act of making love to each other is central to the sacrament.* Just as the sacrament of baptism entails the action of pouring of water, and the sacrament of holy communion entails the action of consuming the consecrated bread and wine, so also the sacrament of marriage entails the action of spouses making love to one another. Properly understood, this lovemaking is much more than a moment of passion: it is a fundamental element in a lifetime of self-giving, generative, and trusting love. The sacrament thus goes on and on in the life of the marriage. For the Church, this total intimacy is a most sacred action, an expression of self-giving love, a God-given love.

The recent Synod on Marriage discussed some of the tensions arising from the Church's rigid stance on sexual ethics and this sacramental understanding of sexual intimacy. Following the Synod, Francis suggested that the Church should be more considerate and pastoral in the guidance it gives on sexual matters: "The complexity of the issues that arose revealed the need for continued open discussion of a number of doctrinal, moral, spiritual, and pastoral questions" and "not all discussions of doctrinal, moral or pastoral issues need to be settled by interventions of the magisterium" (*Amoris Laetitia* 2, 3).

A good pastor, I shall call him Geoffrey because that was his name, ministered to many families. In one of these families, where he had married the parents, baptized the children, married the older children, and buried the grandparents, there was a young woman I shall call Geraldine, though that was not her name. Geoffrey had baptized her and got to know her over the years. Later, as a young adult, Geraldine came up to Geoffrey at another family event. He had not seen her for a few years. "Hello, Geraldine," he said, "what are you up to these days?" "Oh Geoffrey," she said without guile, "I'm living in sin." He replied with a smile and a shake of the head, "I'm sure, Geraldine," he said, "that you would be living in love." He had a pastoral approach. There is confession and absolution here, mercy and encouragement, liberation.

A pastoral approach, however, does not mean "everything goes." The right and the good are not just matters of personal opinion. Love and wisdom may help find a way to the right and the good, without seeming excessive or unbalanced.

7

WHY IS THE CHURCH AGAINST SAME-SEX MARRIAGES?

Pope Francis accepts that young people have "an explicit desire to discuss questions concerning the difference between male and female identity, reciprocity between men and women, and homosexuality" (*Christus Vivit* 81).[1] The Church's stance on members of the LGBTQI+[2] communities may seem uncaring, particularly if young people have gay or lesbian friends or even if they are discovering mysteries in their own sexuality. Widespread publicity of a Vatican Congregation's 2021 ban on priests blessing same-sex unions confirmed these perceptions.[3]

Current Church teaching accepts that some of us are born with same-sex attractions, but formally it judges homosexual acts to be disordered. Francis, however, shows more concern for the person than for the expression of sexuality: "If a person is gay and seeks God and has good will, who am I to judge?"[4] Francis also supports same-sex civil unions, saying "homosexuals...are children of God and have a right to a family." However, he continues to affirm the Church's teaching on marriage, "Marriage is marriage, but this does not mean condemning (homosexual) people," he explained to journalists, "these are our brothers and sisters and we need to be close to them, but marriage as a sacrament is clear."[5]

There are three distinct if overlapping theological issues to consider here. One

---

1. Francis after the Synod on Young People, in *Christus Vivit: Christ is Alive*, where he is also quoting from the pre-synod documentation.

2. The complexity of this acronym serves to remind us of the complexity of human sexualities, and perhaps also of our tendency to exclude what is strange and foreign. The "+" at the end may signify that there is more to consider. It may also suggest the cross.

3. Congregation for the Doctrine of the Faith, regarding the blessing of the unions of persons of the same sex (March 15, 2021).

4. Francis, responding to a journalist's question in a return flight from Brazil, 2013.

5. These quotes, which may suffer in translation, are from the 2020 documentary *Francesco* and a September 2021 interview on a flight from Bratislava to Rome.

has to do with the Church's general teaching in relation to marriage. A second concerns the Church's teaching in relation to same-sex relationships. The third relates to the possibility of the Church's teaching being developed. Let us look at each of these in turn.

~ ◯ ~

First, as discussed in the previous chapter, the Church sees marriage as a replication of the divine love in the Holy Trinity, which is self-giving, intimate, absolute, faithful, fruitful, and eternal. Marriage is therefore something sacred, a visible sign of a divine presence, a sacrament. Furthermore, in the light of key texts in the Bible, from the opening chapters of Genesis and through to the words of Jesus, the Church has taught that marriage pertains to the union of a man and a woman, who are created in the image and likeness of God. The Church's teaching has thus been that "unity, indissolubility, and openness to fertility are essential to marriage" and so "polygamy is incompatible with the unity of marriage; divorce separates what God has joined together; the refusal of fertility turns married life away from its 'supreme gift,' the child" (*Catechism* §1664).

Consequently, the Church has seen marriage as a permanent commitment between a man and a woman for the expression of mutual love and procreation. This has excluded many loving couples. For example, an impotent person cannot marry in the Church because the marriage cannot be biologically consummated. A person who has married in the Church and then been divorced, if their spouse remains alive, cannot marry again in the Church because their relationship is seen neither as a union of male and female nor as open to natural procreation. There are, however, exceptions. Heterosexual couples who are unable to have children, because of infertility, for example, are allowed to marry in the Church and are supported in adopting children as their own.

Perhaps there is room for development in the Church's teaching. Perhaps the personal is more important than the biological. People who have been married for a long time know that the development of a more general physical and spiritual intimacy is key to the joy of love. This includes a trusting openness, a tender innocence, and a doing away with secrets and disguises. It is almost a return to the nakedness of the Garden of Eden, a return to intimacy with God. Could there be room for the inclusion of same-sex relationships in this broader view of marriage?

Perhaps not. Francis carefully reports the findings of the Synod on Marriage:

The Synod Fathers observed that, "as for proposals to place unions between homosexual persons on the same level as marriage, there are absolutely no grounds for considering homosexual unions to be in any way similar or even remotely analogous to God's plan for marriage and family." (*Amoris Laetitia* 251)[6]

Perhaps maybe. Significantly, in the same document, Francis offers his own thoughts about the actual situations in which loving couples find themselves:

There is a need "to avoid judgements which do not take into account the complexity of various situations" and "to be attentive, by necessity, to how people experience distress because of their condition." It is a matter of reaching out to everyone, of needing to help each person find his or her proper way of participating in the ecclesial community....No one can be condemned for ever, because that is not the logic of the Gospel! Here I am not speaking only of the divorced and remarried, but of everyone, in whatever situation they find themselves.[7]

~ ⟲ ~

The Church's teaching in relation to same-sex relationships and LGBTQI+ sexualities is double-sided. On the one hand, the formal teaching is exclusive and harsh; on the other hand, the pastoral practice should be welcoming. Many Church leaders want a Church that is inclusive rather than exclusive. Cardinal Schönborn of Vienna, for example, rejected the 2021 ban of the Congregation for the Doctrine of the Faith on priests blessing same-sex unions because it was deeply wounding and lacked pastoral sensitivity.

The Church has not been alone in marginalizing people with diverse sexualities. The American Association of Psychologists, for example, had listed homosexuality as a "sociopathic personality disturbance" in the 1960s and then as a "sexual disorder not otherwise specified" in 1987. Homosexual acts were considered a criminal offense in many nations. In the United States, for example, such legislation remained on the books until struck down by the Supreme Court in 2003. In India, homosexual activity was listed as a criminal offense up until 2013, and then criminalized again in 2018 because it was "against the order of nature."

---

6. Pope Francis quoting from the final document of the Synod on Marriage (October 24, 2015), no. 76.
7. Pope Francis, *Amoris Laetitia*, nos. 296, 297, quoting from the final document of the Synod on Marriage (2015), no. 51.

Though the Church concedes that many people are same-sex attracted and explicitly condemns "unjust" discrimination against them, it nonetheless appears discriminatory itself. In line with the 1987 statement of the American Association of Psychologists, the Church holds that "homosexual acts are intrinsically disordered" and "do not proceed from a genuine affective and sexual complementarity," and therefore, "under no circumstances can they be approved" (*Catechism* §§2357–58). It might be noted here that no argument or evidence is given to support the judgment that homosexual acts "do not proceed from a genuine affective and sexual complementarity" and that the Church also regards masturbation as an "intrinsically and seriously disordered act."[8] Is there room for reconsideration and development of teaching here?

~ ○ ~

The Church's teaching on marriage and sexuality is based in texts from Sacred Scripture and natural law ethics. There are several verses in the Bible that declare heterosexuality as part of God's creation[9] and reject homosexuality.[10] The teaching therefore seems unchangeable.

However, it is argued by some that these texts may reflect norms of culture—like slavery, polygamy, and patriarchy, which have since been abandoned—rather than the revelation of God. They point to the teaching of the Second Vatican Council, that "the interpreter of Sacred Scripture...should carefully investigate what meaning the sacred writers really intended, and what God wanted to manifest by means of these words" (*Dei Verbum* 12).[11] Perhaps some development of teaching is possible.

Others argue that the application of natural law ethics here ignores the actual complexities of human life and contemporary learnings about psychosexual development. In Australia, for example, 1.7 percent of children born today are anatomically neither clearly male nor clearly female. And, as noted above in chapter 6, the application of the natural law may vary according to circumstances and situations.[12]

Some have urged a positive development of the scope of natural law and the Church's teaching. For example, Lisa Sowle Cahill, professor of theology at Boston College and a specialist in theological ethics, proposes that "shifts in sexual milieus

---

8. Congregation for the Doctrine of the Faith, "Declaration on Certain Questions Concerning Sexual Ethics" (December 29, 1975).

9. See Genesis 1; Mark 10:6; Matthew 19:4.

10. See, e.g., Leviticus 18:22 and 20:13; Romans 1:26–27; 1 Corinthians 6:9–10.

11. Second Vatican Council, Dogmatic Constitution on Divine Revelation, *Dei Verbum* (November 18, 1965). For further reflections on how to read Scripture, see "Why Is the Bible Important?," in John Honner, *Does God Like Being God?*, 9–12.

12. The *Catechism*'s exposition of natural law can be found at §§1954ff.

do not necessarily mean that Christian ethics needs to be re-written entirely, but may require radical reappropriation of the images by which it is formed."[13] She argues that the focus on marriage should be broadened from a focus on sexuality and procreation to include a consideration of family: "In my view, the Christian family is not the nuclear family focused inward on the welfare of its own members but the socially transformative family that seeks to make the Christian moral ideal of love of neighbor part of the common good."[14] Marriages do not merely produce life. They model a way of living.

Francis certainly opens a door for new interpretations of Church teaching on sexuality and marriage when he writes, "Unity of teaching and practice is certainly necessary in the Church, but this does not preclude various ways of interpreting some aspects of that teaching or drawing certain consequences from it" (*Amoris Laetitia* 3).

The Church may come to bless same-sex unions and reduce its opposition to same-sex civil unions. On the one hand, perhaps, following Lisa Sowle Cahill's approach, it will also reflect on marriage and sexuality in the light of the whole gospel and develop its teaching, proclaiming marriage as a gospel-informed commitment to parenting and faithful love. On the other hand, perhaps, in its wisdom and guided by the Holy Spirit, the Church may develop its teaching in another direction. Sometimes, we may humbly have to set aside our own deeply held views. Nevertheless, we can surely hold that the Church should never exclude any among us who are striving to live faithful, creative, and loving lives; and it should never ever cease to celebrate the love of God made flesh among us.

---

13. Lisa Sowle Cahill, *Between the Sexes: Foundations for a Christian Ethics of Sexuality* (Minneapolis: Fortress Press, 1985), 151.
14. Lisa Sowle Cahill, *Family: A Christian Social Perspective* (Minneapolis: Fortress Press, 2000), xi.

8

WHY CAN'T WOMEN BE PRIESTS?

This is a question young people, especially young women, are asking about the Catholic Church. Many may know that women can be priests or ministers in Anglican, Episcopalian, Lutheran, and many other churches. Some may know of the controversial decision to ordain several Catholic women during the communist crackdown on the Catholic Church in Czechoslovakia in 1970.[1] Why are only men given the privilege and power of being ordained? This question may arise out of what Francis called "audacity" of youth. If so, we may need, as he says, to "invest" in it.[2]

At the outset, it should be appreciated that there are many Catholics, including many women, who hold that women have their own unique and important role in the Church, even if not as priests. It is rightly observed that being a priest is not the be-all and end-all of being a Christian. Some see this as a first-world issue for first-world feminists, which may or may not be true, but none of these points are reasons for dismissing the question. Some say the more important issue is to have a "Woman-Church" rather than just demanding that women be given a clerical role.[3] Perhaps we need both Woman-Church and ordained women. Perhaps we need both because while a masculine view of the world tends to divide things into "either/or," a feminine view tends to be "both/and." But what is the Church's teaching on the matter? And where is the Holy Spirit leading us?

John Paul II specifically addressed the ordination of women in his 1994 Apostolic Letter *Ordinatio Sacerdotalis*, on priestly ordination. Reviewing earlier statements of

---

1. The ordaining bishop, who had himself been imprisoned because of his faith for fourteen years, decided to do these ordinations because male priests could not minister to imprisoned and tortured Catholic women, whereas a woman could. The Vatican later declared the ordinations to have been invalid and, in 2007, declared the automatic excommunication of any women and bishops who might participate in such ceremonies.

2. From Pope Francis's exhortation after the Synod on Young People (nos. 232–33), as noted in the introduction to this book.

3. See Rosemary Radford Ruether, "Should Women Want Women Priests or Women-Church?" in *Feminist Theology* 20, no. 1 (2011): 63–72 and subsequent responses. See also her earlier book, *Women-Church* (Eugene OR: Wipf and Stock, 2001).

Paul VI and the Congregation for the Doctrine of the Faith, appealing to the example of Christ who chose his apostles only from among men, and noting the constant practice of the Church, he declared that the exclusion of women from the priesthood is in accordance with God's plan for his Church. He then came to a solemn conclusion:

> In order that all doubt may be removed regarding a matter of great importance, a matter which pertains to the Church's divine constitution itself, in virtue of my ministry of confirming the brethren (cf. Lk 22:32) I declare that the Church has no authority whatsoever to confer priestly ordination on women and that this judgment is to be definitively held by all the Church's faithful. (*Ordinatio Sacerdotalis* 4)

John Paul II, while avoiding the word *infallible*, is explicitly declaring that the ordination of women is not a matter of Church practice or discipline, but, as he states in the opening paragraph of this document, a matter of the Church's constitution, and hence not "open to debate."

This teaching was welcomed by many. Others wondered if the word *definitive* had been improperly used and argued that the Church did have authority to change its teaching on this matter.[4] Some questioned if they could continue to stay in the Church. It seemed to them that the Scripture-based arguments for Jesus only ordaining men as a precedent for all future ordinations were far from constitutive: If Jesus did ordain the twelve at the Last Supper, which is not explicitly stated in the Gospels, and if he only ordained Jews, including married men and a traitor, then could that precedent mean that he only wanted to ordain twelve priests, only Jewish, only men, with some married, and one a traitor?

The early teaching of St. Paul that women were not allowed to speak in churches and should keep silent (see 1 Cor 14:34), may be significant here, but St. Paul had also warmly approved of the work done by Priscilla in instructing Apollos (Acts 18:26). Some say that ordaining women would not be appropriate in more patriarchal Catholic communities in the developing world, and that it would also set back communion with Eastern Orthodox churches. Others counter by saying that not ordaining women would alienate many women from the Church in the developed world and would set back communion with Protestant churches.

---

4.   These are esoteric arguments. For measured treatments of both sides of the arguments, see Richard Gaillardetz, "Infallibility and the Ordination of Women," *Louvain Studies* 21 (1996): 3–24; and Avery Dulles, "Gender and Priesthood: Examining the Teaching," *Origins* 25, no. 45 (1996). For a broader study, see Phyllis Zagano, *Women and Catholicism: Gender, Communion and Authority* (New York: Palgrave Macmillan, 2011).

The bishops at the Synod on Young People accepted that the role of women in the Church remained an issue, particularly for young people:

A Church that seeks to live a synodal style cannot fail to reflect on the condition and role of women within it, and consequently in society more generally. Young men and women ask this question forcefully....A sphere of particular importance in this regard is the female presence in ecclesial bodies at all levels, including positions of responsibility, as well as female participation in ecclesial decision-making processes, respecting the role of the ordained minister.[5]

Francis, when asked in 2016 about the ordination of women in the Catholic Church, had replied that "John Paul II had the last clear word on this and it stands, this stands." When then asked if this clear word would stand forever, he answered, "If we read carefully the declaration by St. John Paul II, it is going in that direction." Perhaps this is a subtle reply, because Francis seems to be changing directions, if ever so slightly. In 2016, he created a commission to study the ordination of women as deacons. One of the members of that commission, Phyllis Zagano, notes,

The Catholic Churches most assuredly have ordained women as deacons... with virtually identical ceremonies to those they used for the men they ordained as deacons...women deacons primarily ministered to women: women deacons assisted at baptism, catechized women and children, provided spiritual direction to women, heard their confessions, brought them the Eucharist, and anointed them in illness and death.[6]

Although the commission did not reach an agreement, Francis did not let the matter rest there. In 2020, he established a new commission to study the same matter again, with completely new if perhaps less expert membership. Furthermore, in 2021, he changed the Church's liturgical law to allow women to be formally admitted into what used to be called the "minor orders" of lector and acolyte. The direction seems to be changing, if ever so slightly.

These steps may not be enough to persuade young women, who feel they are called to the priesthood, to abide in a Church that excludes them from the priesthood

---

5. Synod of Bishops on Young People, Final Document, "Young People, the Faith and Vocational Discernment" (October 27, 2018), no. 148.

6. Phyllis Zagano, *Women: Icons of Christ* (Mahwah, NJ: Paulist Press, 2020), 3–4.

because of their gender. What comfort can be given them? One might suggest that, like St. Ignatius Loyola, they humbly accept the authority of the papacy. Or they might point to Dorothy Day, who accepted the authority of the Church even when it meant she had to separate from the love of her life. These kinds of responses, however, may only deepen wounds and perpetuate the disorder of gendered authority in the Church.

A more fruitful approach might entail understanding the exercise of the priesthood as being neither male nor female, but *in persona Christi*—in the person of Christ. In Catholic Tradition, the priest is understood to take the place of Christ, the risen Lord. In Christ Jesus the risen Lord, as St. Paul says, there is neither male nor female (see Gal 3:28). The priest is thus in the person of Christ but not in the gender of Jesus. That is why priests wear vestments, almost to camouflage their own personalities. A priest friend, both holy and infuriating, understood this point deeply. He followed the words and rubrics of the Missal exactly. He never introduced himself as Father Paul. He never added a touch of his own personality. He never told stories about himself in his preaching. He barely made eye contact with the congregation. He took his watch off before he went to the altar. The Mass became a moment in the eternity of the risen Lord. He humbled himself *in persona Christi*.

While most of us would probably prefer a more personal priestly presence, given the mess of our own lives, with the priest sharing our humanity, I very much accept my friend's point about the priest acting *in persona Christi*. Zagano takes this approach further, pointing out that the persona of Christ is the persona of a servant, not the persona of a male.[7] If we accept acting *in persona Christi* as crucial to the exercise of priesthood, then we can gather as one in Christ Jesus, male and female. It is to this that we are called. This mystical union sometimes seems a long road ahead. And sometimes it happens right before our eyes.

---

7. Zagano, *Women: Icons of Christ*, 3.

9

WHY CAN'T PRIESTS BE MARRIED?

This question might come from a young person who wants to be a priest but also wants to be married. It might even come from someone who wants to marry a priest. Or it might come from someone who is married and who feels called to the priesthood. Most probably, however, it arises because young people find it weird that priests aren't allowed to marry or don't want to marry. You could suggest that the LGBTQI+ communities could add the letter C for celibates, who today are also somewhat marginalized because of their sexuality. More seriously, you could suggest that we also need to talk about what it means to be a priest in the Church, and not solely about priestly celibacy.

The usual answer as to why priests can't be married today is relatively simple. Over the centuries, the Church had found that celibacy helped priests draw closer to Christ and then later formally decreed, as a matter of law, that priests can neither marry nor be married. However, unlike the teaching that prevents the ordination of women, the practice of priestly celibacy is not claimed to be constitutive of the faith. The law can be changed.

The longer answer about celibacy is not so simple. In Jewish tradition, priests had to be married, because they were descended from the tribe of Levi. Their fathers were usually either priests or in some other service in the temple. Their sons followed the same path. And yet, Scripture has special respect for single holy women and men, like Ruth, Jeremiah, Anna, John the Baptist, and Jesus, none of whom were priests of the temple. St. Paul was not a priest, but he said he was celibate because "the unmarried man is anxious about the affairs of the Lord, how to please the Lord; but the married man is anxious about the affairs of the world, how to please his wife" (1 Cor 7:32–34). In defense of the married apostles, however, he elsewhere wrote, "Do we not have the right to be accompanied by a believing wife, as do the other apostles and the brothers of the Lord and Cephas [Peter]" (1 Cor 9:5). In a later writing of the

New Testament, in the first letter to Timothy, we read that "a bishop must be...married only once" and "let deacons be married only once" (1 Tim 3:2, 12).

The longer answer about the nature of the priesthood is equally complicated and equally instructive. In the Gospels, the only references to priests are about the priests of the temple and the synagogues, and the Greek word used for them is *hiereus*, from which we get the word *hierarchy*. Jesus says nothing about being a priest himself nor about his followers being priests. In the early writings of St. Paul, we find no mention of priests. Neither his list of the many roles given to individual members of the Church (Rom 12:6–8), nor his list of the variety of services in the Church (1 Cor 12:8–10), includes priests or elders. We read about deacons, priests, and bishops only in the later writings of the New Testament, notably Acts and Timothy, although the Greek word translated as "priest" is not *hiereus* but *presbuteros*—from which we get the words *presbytery* and *priest*. It seems the priests of the early Christian community were imagined quite differently from the priests of the temple.

The threefold structure of deacons, priests, and bishops was soon firmly established in the early Church. For example, St. Ignatius of Antioch, who died in the year 106, described the bishop as being in the place of God and watching over the Church; the priests as being in the place of the apostles and forming a kind of college that leads the churches; and the deacons as serving the people, including dispensing the sacraments. While these developments may not have been explicitly set out by Jesus, they are taken to be confirmed by the Spirit that Jesus had promised he would send to guide the growing Church.

For the first thousand years of the Christian Church there was no general law against priests being married, although celibacy was in some places recommended and in other places imposed. During the Middle Ages, as the great monasteries developed, many young men were drawn into religious life with its vows of chastity and obedience. This was seen as a higher and more effective way of following Christ.

Celibacy gradually became the norm for all priests. In 1123, the First Lateran Council prohibited priests from living with their wives. In 1139, the Second Lateran Council prohibited priests from marrying after they had been ordained. In the following centuries and through various measures, including depriving married priests of income and property and the wherewithal to raise a family, it became increasingly rare for priests to be married. In 1563, the Council of Trent formally prohibited priests from being married and set up seminaries for the training of young men to be priests. In 1917, mandatory celibacy was enshrined in the Church's Canon Law.

It is important to note here that there is a difference between the mandated celibacy for Catholic priests and the vow of chastity taken by members of religious communities. Religious vows have different origins and a different significance. In the early centuries of the Christian Church, there were communities of monks and nuns who moved into the desert and took vows of chastity as central to their following the way of Jesus. Today, this tradition of religious life is continued by Benedictines, Franciscans, Dominicans, Jesuits, Salesians, Marists, Josephites, and many other religious institutes and associations. These men and women all take vows of chastity, but not all of them are priests.

Some argue that priestly celibacy was imposed because a sexually active priest was seen as an "impure" person unworthy to celebrate the Eucharist. Others argue that celibacy was only imposed to prevent Church money and property being bequeathed to a priest's family. Most, however, observe that the Church found that celibacy, while difficult, can bring a priest closer to Jesus and closer to God. Karl Rahner, while in many ways a keen reformer, saw celibacy as "a holy tradition of ancient evangelic wisdom... swimming against the stream...professing the folly of the cross."[1] John Paul II similarly wrote that "celibacy is a priceless gift of God for the Church and has a prophetic value for the world today" (*Pastores Dabo Vobis* 29).

The priceless gift, unfortunately, does come at a cost when it is made mandatory. The Australian Royal Commission into Institutional Responses to Child Sexual Abuse found that compulsory celibacy "contributed to the occurrence of sexual abuse, especially when combined with other risk factors." While it acknowledged "that only a minority of Catholic clergy and religious have sexually abused children," it recommended that "the Holy See consider introducing voluntary celibacy for diocesan clergy."[2]

The Church has the power to change the law of celibacy. At the 2019 Synod on the Amazon, Francis approved the discussion of ordaining married men where there was a shortage of priests and unmet pastoral needs. He admitted his own view, though, was "that celibacy is a gift to the church." Nonetheless, married priests from Anglican or Lutheran Churches, and who choose to become Catholics, today can remain married after their ordination in the Roman Catholic Church. Furthermore, priests in some Catholic communities, such as the Maronite and Ukrainian Catholic

---

1. Karl Rahner, *Servants of the Lord* (New York: Herder, 1968), 168.

2. The Australian Royal Commission into Institutional Responses to Child Sexual Abuse, *Final Report*, vol. 16, Religious Institutions 1 (Barton, AU: Attorney-General Department, 2017), 46–47.

Churches, can be married prior to being ordained and continue in both priestly service and married life.

Given that the Church has been guided by the Holy Spirit through the centuries as the role of the priesthood has been both developed and reformed, we can expect that the Spirit will urge us on to further development and reform.

A PERSONAL POSTSCRIPT ON MARRIED PRIESTS

I know many married priests in other Christian churches who fulfill the roles of husband or wife and, at the same time, the role of priest and pastor. I know of married priests who have come from other churches and been welcomed into the Catholic Church while also continuing in their marriage. And I know many married people who work in equally if not more demanding ministries—for example school principals, doctors, and politicians—who manage, often with some difficulty, to carry out the dual roles of ministry and marriage.

Having been active as a priest for more than twenty years, and then married for more than twenty years—not both at the same time—I have some experience of the blessings and demands in both states of life. Both entail self-giving love. In marriage, one not only gives love but also receives love in return. In the priesthood, in my experience, there is also much self-giving love and often the consolation of being united with Jesus, but not so much love is directly experienced in return—despite best efforts and rare exceptions. A close understanding companion, as St. Paul noted, would certainly help.

The current duties and expectations of a Catholic priest would certainly challenge a marriage. I doubt that I could have been the kind of priest I was—which meant walking alongside all kinds of people at all times of the day and night—and be married at the same time. I doubt that I could have given the same level of care to the communities I served and at the same time create a community of love with my wife. This is not to say that all priests should be celibate, but to recognize the issues and to explore the possibility of different models of priesthood. Now, as an older and wiser person, I think I can help the community in reflecting on the gospel and celebrating the sacraments, if not in administration or some of the more demanding works of pastoral care.

Having a married clergy would almost certainly increase vocations to ministry and augment seminary training for ministry. There are many ordained clergy in

Protestant Churches whose parents were ministers and whose children later become ministers. Each generation built on the example and wisdom of their elders. There could be no better inspiration or formation for ministry. I continue to hope that the roles of the priest and the rules for celibacy will once again be revised. It is a special vocation.

10

HOW CAN I KNOW MY VOCATION?

R ichard Gill—from a boisterous Catholic family, with a shock of white hair, impish grin, many orchestras, thousands of students, and a love of opera and jive—was a greatly admired Australian educator and conductor. He had a remarkable gift for remembering everyone's name. He was once speaking with a fifteen-year-old prodigy who, in real humility, was worried about whether or not he should strive to become a concert pianist. Richard said to him something like this: "I am a good pianist. I wanted to be a concert pianist, but I found I didn't quite have that gift. I found I loved teaching. That was my gift. But you, my boy, the angel of God has touched you lightly on the shoulder with her finger. You have that rarest of gifts. The music comes out of you." He was helping a young person find their vocation not just in terms of achievement, but also in terms of their spirit. Vocation has something to do with our unique talents and genes. More than this, though, it is a spiritual force that urges us to do something with our talent and genes for the good of others.

The 2018 Catholic Church Synod of Bishops on Young People had a predetermined agenda, namely, "young people, the faith and vocational discernment." At first sight, this looked like a thinly disguised project to promote vocations to the priesthood and religious life. The young people who attended the pre-synodal meeting, however, were more interested in a bigger picture. "We seek a Church that helps us find our vocation," they said, "in all of its senses."[1] Young Catholics had also reported that mental health issues were at the top of the list of their concerns.[2] I suspect there is a connection between vocation and mental health, because both are about our spirit, about finding our place, our purpose in life, about feeling loved and gifted and called.

There was a time in the Catholic Church when *vocation* meant a special calling to a "higher" state of life as a priest or a vowed religious sister or brother. "In all of its

---

1. See the final document from the pre-synodal meeting of more than three hundred young people convened in Rome in 2018.
2. See, e.g., *Called to Fullness of Life and Love*, the Australian Catholic Bishops' Youth Survey (Canberra: ACBC, 2017), 38–40.

senses," however, vocation has a more general meaning—our calling in life. Francis says vocation is a calling with a purpose, and ultimately, it is "a calling from a friend, who is Jesus...as a call to missionary service to others" (*Christus Vivit* 287, 253). The Presbyterian theologian Frederick Buechner offers a similar but more evocative description of vocation: "The place God calls you to is the place where your deep gladness and the world's deep hunger meet."[3]

Imagine a young person on the threshold of life from a well-to-do family—a young person who has a sense of God and who wants to live a good life. And this fine young person asks you, "What am I to do with my life?" or "Do you think I have a vocation?"

There was such a young person in the Gospels. We do not know his name. He ran up to Jesus and knelt before him and said, "Good Teacher, what must I do to inherit eternal life?" (Mark 10:17). Jesus did not answer him immediately. Rather, Jesus looked deeply at him, as if to see his heart, to see if he was boasting or telling the truth. And then the Gospel tells us that Jesus loved him, as if recognizing the young man's spirit and seeing he really was telling the truth. The young man said he wanted to inherit eternal life. Jesus tells him to sell what he owns, give the money to the poor, discover a different kind of treasure, and follow him. This is a big ask for any young person. The young man, as the Gospel tells us, "was shocked and went away grieving, for he had many possessions" (v. 22).

It is a great honor when a young person asks us for advice, especially if it is about the big decisions in life. This may include considering a calling to religious life or the priesthood. It may entail leaving home. It can be a particularly difficult time. Like Jesus, we should not answer immediately, but rather, as the Gospel puts it, we should look into their heart and love them. Can we sense what is driving them? Like Richard Gill, can we help them recognize their unique gifts and deep desires? Can we help them see that an angel has touched them? Can we help them see that their sole vocation is to be the unique person that God created them to be, a perfect fit for their entire life that will bring both challenges and deep joy? We may need to be patient and loving.

Some young people are given rare gifts. Sometimes they must make very difficult decisions. It helps to be a spiritual person if we are going to be able to help young people find their own unique spirit. We might explain to them that the good spirit does not come as a transactional voice that says, "If you do this for me, then I will

---

3. Frederick Buechner, *Wishful Thinking: A Theological ABC* (New York: HarperCollins, 1993), 118–19.

do that for you." Rather, the call of God is gentle and quietly persistent, and the call fills us with a deep consolation that can only be the touch of God's angel. God's call demands discernment. Francis puts it this way:

> Discernment is always done in the presence of the Lord, looking at the signs, listening to the things that happen, the feeling of the people, especially the poor....I am always wary of decisions made hastily. I am always wary of the first decision, that is, the first thing that comes to my mind if I have to make a decision. This is usually the wrong thing. I have to wait and assess, looking deep into myself, taking the necessary time. The wisdom of discernment redeems the necessary ambiguity of life.[4]

Richard Gill died from cancer in October 2018. He spent his last days at home, confined to his bed. When word went out that he was close to death, the principal trumpeter of the Sydney Symphony Orchestra decided to arrange a spontaneous concert. A crowd of musicians assembled in the street outside Richard's house, from flautist Jane Rutter to the Police Brass Band. They played Richard's favorite piece, "The Dam Busters March," and then broke out into applause. Inside the house Richard opened his eyes and smiled. He had helped so many to find their vocation, and he was on the way to finding his ultimate vocation.

4. Antonio Spadaro, "A Big Heart Open to God: An interview with Pope Francis," *America*, September 30, 2013, https://www .americamagazine.org/faith/2013/09/30/big-heart-open-god-interview-pope-francis.

11

WHY DO YOU NEED THAT TALL HAT?

A beautiful girl from Singapore called Faith, aged eight, asked this question in a letter to Pope Francis. She included a drawing of herself with the Pontiff, she with her ponytail hair flying in the wind, and he, almost smiling, with a big miter balanced on top of his head. He replied, "My tall hat is the symbol or sign that I am a bishop. I put it on for some special occasions and during Mass."[1]

Faith's question might suggest that, for a child, a tall hat looks odd, perhaps reminiscent of the so-called Mad Hatter in *Alice in Wonderland*. Her question reminded me of a teenager from Wollongong who could not understand why priests wore what he called "really weird outfits." It could be noted that many celebrities in youth culture seem to thrive on "really weird" outfits, but that would be a distraction.

Headwear is often a sign of office and function. The more important the office, the more elaborate the headwear. Kings and queens wear crowns to reflect their consecration and heritage. Judges wear wigs to indicate they are venerable and acting impersonally. Pilots put on peaked caps, perhaps to make planes fly better. Police wear braided caps to show their authority. Cyclists wear helmets so they won't get hurt if they fall over. Men wear top hats to look important. Women wear beautiful hats to celebrate great social occasions. And last but not least, Russian grenadiers wore a miter, because it is much easier to throw a hand grenade when your hat doesn't have a brim. These may also be some of the reasons why bishops, and particularly the bishops of Rome, wear a tall hat.

You won't find much about hats or vestments in the Gospels, or even in the whole Bible, though there are reports of the Lord God's lengthy instructions for the sons of Aaron to wear "sacred vestments" including a turban and a sash made of "gold, blue, purple and crimson yarns, and fine linen...for their glorious adornment...

---

1. See Pope Francis, *Dear Pope Francis: The Pope Answers Letters from Children around the World* (Chicago: Loyola Press, 2016), 60–61.

so that they may serve me as priests" (Exod 28). Jesus, however, had little time for special clothes.[2] Only after he was taken into captivity was he forced to wear a purple robe and a crown of thorns.

There is a scene in the Acts of the Apostles, on the day of Pentecost, where the Holy Spirit comes like the sound of a rushing wind among the apostles and tongues of fire rest on each of them. I had always thought that a bishop's miter was a symbol of this presence of the Holy Spirit in the leadership of the Church. During the Australian Government's inquiry into the institutional abuse of children, which exposed so many failures of compassion and authority in the Catholic Church, it was mooted that the bishops might set aside their miters for twelve months as an acknowledgment of their failure to follow the Holy Spirit and a sign of humility and repentance.

This might have been a good idea, but in fact, the miter was not intended to be the symbol of the presence of the Holy Spirit. It began life as the Greek word *mitra*, which originally meant a piece of armor, then a headband, and then later was used to translate "turban." The miter evolved out of the tiara, a kind of crown worn by popes since the tenth century, which had begun life as a conical felt hat worn by the emancipated slaves of ancient Rome. How things change.

Tiaras and miters became more and more precious and elaborate until, after his coronation in 1963, Paul VI put the bejeweled triple tiara aside as a "renunciation of human glory and power" and instructed that it be sold and the money given to the poor. The tiara has since then disappeared from the papal coat of arms and wardrobe. The tall hat remains.

Over the centuries, the miter appears to have become taller and taller. Very rarely, however, does it look convincing. As an Anglican theologian and minister tellingly put it,

> Mitres are singularly unflattering. I have met a bishop on whom the mitre didn't look completely daft—but it was a long time ago, and said bishop has long retired. On most people they just look daft....To most, and I would suggest especially the young, the sight of bishops in mitres puts them in another world. It is a world of the past, a world of nostalgia, a world of deference—and mostly a world which is quite disconnected from present experience and values. It confirms for many the impression of a church irrelevant to modern questions, contained in its own bubble of self reference. And in its hierarchical understanding of authority, it is a culture of

---

2. See John Honner, *Did Jesus Have a Girlfriend?*, chap. 4, "What Did Jesus Look Like? What Did He wear?"

which contemporary society is becoming less and less tolerant, possibly for good reason.[3]

I suspect this is what young Faith, consciously or unconsciously, may have been wondering about. Perhaps we might continue to use a smaller traditional miter, that belongs to a diocese rather than to a bishop, for their ordination and installment and for the most solemn of official functions, but—please—could bishops not wear a miter for every smiling episcopal photo opportunity? In *Alice in Wonderland* we get the same advice: "Take off your hat," the King said to the Hatter. "It isn't mine," said the Hatter.

3. Ian Paul, "Why Bishops Should Throw Away Their Mitres," Psephizo blog, July 5, 2017, https://www.psephizo.com/life-ministry/why-bishops-should-throw-away-their-mitres/.

12

WHY DO WE HAVE TO GO TO CHURCH? IT'S SO BORING!

Here is a story about big church and little church. Yuri came to stay with us for the weekend. We were giving his mother a break. He's a good, smart kid. Well organized. Loves competing in games. We played a strange war game, then Scrabble (he could use his online Scrabble dictionary), and then Monopoly. At the end of the day, he asked, "What are we going to do tomorrow?" "Well," I said, "normally we go to Church on Sunday morning." The conversation then went like this:

"Why?"

"To give thanks to God for the wonder of life and for all of creation. And to be part of a bigger community."

He looked thoughtful. I was thoughtful too. It was COVID-19 pandemic time. I counted among the vulnerable. We didn't have to go to Church. I had an idea.

"We could go to little church or big church."

"What's little church?"

"Little church is inside a church building. God is there."

"What's big church?"

"Big church is going out on a kayak into the middle of the ocean and singing hymns. God is there too."

"Can we go to big church?"

Pittwater is a beautiful harbor just north of Sydney, with a national park on one side and, on the other side, a sprinkling of houses among trees above small golden beaches. We set out in a two-seater kayak with Yuri at the front. It was a perfectly glorious morning. Suddenly, without a word from me, Yuri started singing a hymn in a true and gentle voice. And then he went onto the second verse. I said nothing. A little further on, he started singing another hymn. He understood big church. Yuri loved big church. I thought of Jesus's response to the Samaritan woman, who had asked him whether she should worship God in the temple or on the mountain. Jesus replied,

> Woman, believe me, the hour is coming when you will worship the Father neither on this mountain nor in Jerusalem...the hour is coming, and is now here, when the true worshipers will worship the Father in spirit and truth, for the Father seeks such as these to worship him. God is spirit, and those who worship him must worship in spirit and truth. (John 4:21–24)

"Why do we have to go to Church?" This, and the other tiresome questions that children often ask—"Are we there yet?", "What's for dinner?", "Why do I have to eat my vegetables?", and "Why do I have to practice my music again?"—are all connected. This is because they are all about growing up. Going to Church—even more than vegetables or music practice—is good for us! It gives us a compass, a community, a meaning, and a purpose. Just as going to a gym regularly helps us grow our bodies, going to a Church regularly helps us grow our souls:

> In the past 20 years, there has been escalating research focusing on the relationships between various dimensions of religiosity and mental health. To date, several thousand studies demonstrate positive associations between the two. Results indicate that those who are more religious generally fare better in terms of mental health....Higher religiosity has also been associated with lower rates of suicide, reduced prevalence of drug and alcohol misuse, and reduced delinquency.[1]

We could say that going to Church is what we do in our family because we are followers of Jesus. Some negotiation might be required. Parents might acknowledge that adolescence is a time of growing as an individual and making personal choices, but at the same time hold that family is important and adolescents are not yet independent adults. Perhaps surprisingly, research shows that the good example of parents is a stronger influence on young people than peer pressure.[2]

---

1. Simon Dein, "Against the Stream: Religion and Mental Health," *BJPsych Bull* 42, no. 3 (2018). See also the notes on the relationships between religion and well-being in chap. 2 above, "Doesn't religion do more harm than good?"

2. As noted by Professor Maree Teesson, director of the Matilda Centre for Research in Mental Health and Substance Use, University of Sydney, "Rising ICE Use in Australia and the Latest Research on Treatments," June 2021, in *On Health Report with Dr. Norman Swan*, produced by Sarah Sedghi, ABC podcasts, 14:56, https://www.abc.net.au/radionational/programs/healthreport/rising-ice-use-in-australia/13681400.

None of these responses, however, focuses on the other side of the problem. Perhaps young people find Mass boring because to them it feels as though it has nothing to do with their world. Young people are at their lowest functioning level in the morning, but that is when we mostly celebrate the Mass. Young people are sensitive about criticism, yet we start the Mass by declaring ourselves to be grievous sinners. We give them Scripture readings that are often unintelligible and poorly read. We give them a sexist and barely English transliteration of a Latin liturgy that itself includes poor translations of the original Hebrew and Greek. The Mass is meant to be a holy drama that reveals God's loving presence, but it rarely seems that way.

The Mass is not meant to be entertaining. Jesus was not interested in entertaining people. The miracles were not part of a circus act. Many walked away from Jesus because he demanded more of them. But Jesus did engage with people. He walked with them. He spoke their language. He told parables that related to their lives. He spoke with authority. He was nothing if not authentic. He was not boring. We don't have to pander to young people, but we need to listen to them. The Mass could be far more engaging.

There are great models of youth Masses that work well, where creative pastors take risks and wise bishops turn a blind eye, but alas, these are exceptions. Again, many Catholic high schools arrange engaging liturgies, though sometimes it can be hard to find a priest who is willing to go with their flow, and sometimes they will be criticized for "going too far" by having young people "preach" or allowing non-Catholic students to receive communion. We could link schools and parishes in many creative ways.

In conclusion, why do we have to go to Mass on Sundays? It is not enough to say that it is a command of the Church. Christians participate in Sunday Mass to remember the important things in life, so that we can be nurtured, and so that we can grow in love. Only with Jesus's living presence within us and among us can we continue his mission.

A POSTSCRIPT ON CHURCH TEACHING ON SUNDAY OBLIGATION

In the Bible, God makes a solemn contract with Abraham and his descendants. Their covenant is sealed with blood sacrifices and later codified in the Ten Commandments. The third of these commandments, high up on the pecking order, is:

"Remember the sabbath day, and keep it holy" (Exod 20:8). We are told that Jesus "went to the synagogue on the sabbath day, as was his custom" (Luke 4:16).

Jesus blesses bread and wine and shares it among his disciples. He calls this action "the new covenant in my blood," and he tells his disciples to "do this in remembrance of me." And so it was, as we read in the Acts of the Apostles, that the early Christians gathered "on the first day of the week...to break bread" (Acts 20:7).

The practice of sharing in the Eucharist on a Sunday, the day of the Lord's resurrection, also became a custom rather than a law. The obligation to attend Mass on Sundays only became a formal rule of the Church in the Code of Canon Law promulgated in 1917. The updated Code now reads, "On Sundays and other holy days of obligation, the faithful are obliged to participate in the Mass" (Can. §1247). The *Catechism* adds that "those who deliberately fail in this obligation commit a grave sin" (§2181).

There is much commentary on these regulations. Some ask what constitutes a serious reason for not going to Mass. Others wonder what kind of deliberate failure constitutes a grave sin. Pope Francis, who is usually very pastoral in his reflection on Church law, takes a firm stance on Sunday obligation. He doesn't talk about how we sin by missing Mass, however, but about what we gain by attending Mass. He says,

> Sunday is a holy day for us, sanctified by the Eucharistic celebration, the living presence of the Lord among us and for us. Thus, it is the Mass that *makes* Sunday Christian. The Christian Sunday revolves around the Mass. For a Christian, what is a Sunday in which the encounter with the Lord is lacking?...How can we practice the Gospel without drawing the energy necessary to do so, one Sunday after another, from the inexhaustible source of the Eucharist? We do not go to Mass in order to give something to God, but *to receive what we truly need from him.*[3]

In other words, he is saying that we are obliged to go to Mass because it is essential for our own good. For those of us on pilgrimage in the caravan of the Church, the Eucharist is like a *caravanserai*—a roadside resting place—for our nourishment and restoration.

---

3. Pope Francis, General Audience, Rome (December 13, 2017). (Italics in original.)

13

WHY CAN'T THE MASS ALWAYS BE LIKE THAT?

W e were a long way from home, staying with a younger friend who was living in a city on the East Coast of the United States. She does much to help the Church serve the poor, she respects many people in the Church, but she finds the public face of the Church unwelcoming and inauthentic. We had taken her to a Sunday morning Mass at a nearby parish. The streets were eerily bare and there were traffic control barriers on every corner. It turned out that this was the morning of the Pride March.

The Church was venerable, smelling of wax, a combination of light and dark. I can't remember if we were welcomed or not, but there was an order of service with readings and hymns in Spanish and English. A man was playing contemplatively on a grand piano near the sanctuary. We knelt and prayed. People gathered. The church started to fill. A dignified woman, vested in an alb, prepared the altar. The sanctuary was uncluttered, the lighting gentle, almost mystical. There was an unfussy reverence. The Mass began with what turned out to be a very appropriate hymn, "All Are Welcome." We sang alternate verses in English and Spanish. The music was simple, elegant, engaging. By this time, the church was half-full—old, young, families, and solitary.

The priest welcomed everyone. He acknowledged that the Pride March would be beginning soon, linking the divine liturgy with social reality. The readings alternated between English and Spanish. The priest sat down for his homily, just as Jesus used to sit down when he taught the people. He was not long-winded. He opened up the Word of God. During the Eucharistic Prayer a dozen women and men—servers, readers, cantors, collectors, and musicians—came up from among the people and stood together around the altar as a microcosm of the whole community, even of the whole cosmos.

Before the final blessing at the end of the Mass, the priest explained that some members of the congregation were about to join the Pride March. He invited them—some old, some young, some couples, some families—to stand for a blessing and support. They stood shyly, slightly huddled, as if feeling vulnerable. The rest of the congregation stood too, joining hands in a prayer for them. The marchers were much moved by this support coming from the community. One man near us was almost heaving with emotion. This was a whole communion.

There was a final hymn, some silence, and then some quiet chatter. It was a perfectly ordinary and orthodox Mass. We spoke briefly with the priest, who was waiting outside the main entrance to the church. He seemed a shy man, far from charismatic, yet authentic. Our younger friend was close to tears, feeling this connection between the Church and the hopes and struggles that real people have in their lives. That was when she asked her question: "Why can't the Mass always be like that?"

14

WHY DOES THE CHURCH OPPOSE ABORTION AND EUTHANASIA?

These are pressing and controversial questions. They are about birth and death, the important things in life. The Church is about birth and death too, and it is intending to defend the absolute value of every human life. Its stances on abortion and euthanasia, however, appear rigid and negative to many, particularly to those who defend individual rights and especially women's reproductive rights. The Church is in the paradoxical position of defending life yet seeming to lack compassion for people who find themselves in excruciating situations in their own lives.

The first response we should make to a young person asking this question might be to explore why they are asking it, and what their concerns are. This is because it might relate to a difficult family situation for some young people. More careful listening might be called for. For others it might be a more general question.

In general, a short answer to this question might be that, because the Church believes life to be the most precious of God-given gifts, it opposes any and every action deliberately intended to take a life, including war, the death penalty, and disproportionate self-defense (see *Catechism* §§2318–30). That is why it also opposes abortion and euthanasia. Given that the Church's purpose is to continue Jesus's mission to the world, which is about the fullness of life, then it is also called to speak up on these issues in the public forum.

But surely, a young person might ask, can there be exceptions to these rules? What if a young girl is pregnant because of a vicious assault? Or what if a much-loved grandfather has been anxiously struggling for breath day after day? And hasn't the Church made exceptions about wars that were considered to be just, or a death penalty that was warranted, or self-defense that demanded a lethal response? And what of the role of personal conscience?

Catholic teaching permits exceptions when the intention of an action is not to take a life deliberately. For example, a surgeon may ethically operate on a pregnant woman to remove a lethal cancer from her uterus, even though this may risk the life of her child. This is because the proposed action is not intended to take a life. Or again, every possible step may be taken to relieve a dying person of pain, even "at the risk of shortening their days" (*Catechism* §§2258–79). The intention is to relieve pain, not to kill. This is called the principle of double effect. It does not imply that the end justifies the means, and it does not allow intentional taking of a life, but it does allow for a good action that might entail a risk of death, provided that the intention is good and the actions are proportionate.

Longer answers get more complicated. One considerable issue in the debates about abortion and euthanasia is that the protagonists begin from completely different starting points. The Church's teaching about abortion, for example, is based on three principles that many who hold an opposing view would find somewhat esoteric and abstract. First, as well understood by people of faith, Scripture affirms that from its beginning human life involves the creative action of God and, because life is sacred, one of the Ten Commandments is "You shall not kill." Second, and resting on a particular view of biology, human life is considered to begin precisely at the moment of conception. And third, arguing from natural law ethics, the Church holds that "the inalienable right to life of every innocent human individual is a constitutive element of a civil society and its legislations." Therefore, "abortion willed either as an end or a means, is gravely contrary to the moral law." The Church holds that "this teaching has not changed and will not change" (*Catechism* §§2258, 2270, 2771, 2273).

The Church values every human person because she or he can love and be loved—not because of their brilliance, prowess, or wealth—and without any exceptions. There is something very positive and countercultural in the Church taking the side of the innocent and powerless in civil debates, particularly in matters of life and death. Furthermore, these abstract and rational elements of the Church's ethics should be considered in the light of its complementary teaching about the "right to act in conscience and in freedom so as personally to make moral decisions" and its recognition that there are "situations that make moral judgments less assured and decision difficult" (*Catechism* §§1782, 1787).[1]

Advocates for legal termination of pregnancy and voluntary assisted dying tend to argue from more existential and contemporary starting points. They seem to show

---

1. A good conscience is well informed and guided by the Church's teaching (*Catechism* §§1783–85), and "a human being must always obey the certain judgement of his [or her] conscience" (§1800).

more concern for the actual situations of suffering that people find themselves in. They speak more about rights than about natural law, particularly about women's reproductive rights and the rights of a dying person to have a say in how they will die. They are concerned with caring for a suffering person immediately present to them. They are not likely to be swayed by appeals to Scripture, outdated biology, or natural law ethics. The beginnings and endings of life are measured differently. There are some apparent inconsistencies in their ethics, given that abortion is not seen as taking a life and euthanasia is about taking a life, but utilitarian ethics is more concerned with situations than with consistency. It can change.

The gap between the protagonists in these debates, sadly, has become so large that there is more labeling than listening, more recrimination than respect, more finger-pointing than embracing. People are drawing battle lines rather than building bridges. Positions have become politicized. None of this befits Christians, who are called to love their enemies. People should not be condemned if they are trying to protect life, and people should not be judged when they are trying to alleviate suffering or trying to make the right choice in very difficult existential situations. Generations of women have been disregarded and affronted, yet women are at least as capable as men, if not more capable, in making ethical decisions.

There is some common ground, fortunately, in the shared urge to care for suffering people with compassion and to support them as a community. Common ground can also be found in the protection of innocent children, the abolition of the death penalty, and the ending of the arms race. Perhaps, as noted previously in chapter 6, the application of the natural law may be reconsidered in some cases. Perhaps the starting and ending points of human life might be judged not just on biology, but also on what it means to be a person. Biologically, the moment of conception seems critical, but in personal terms a human life may begin later. It may also begin earlier, when a couple makes a loving commitment to each other and to a future family. Perhaps the sexual revolution has taken society beyond a healthy point of balance, where sex has come to be seen as more about self-satisfaction and recreation than about self-giving and procreation. Dialogue on these concerns should continue. Surely the primacy of intentions to protect life, to offer mercy, and to alleviate suffering can be recognized. Certainly, much can be done to improve palliative care of the dying so that their suffering can be taken away, even if at the risk of shortening their days.

In the end, we might say to a young person that Christians should always be on the side of life, whether the life of an individual, the life of a community, or the life of the planet. For this reason, the Church should always be opposed to violence of all kinds: not only to the death penalty and warfare, but also to disproportionate use of guns, to racism, to barriers to refugees, to inequality of wealth and health, and to the neglect of the poor. The Church may not always align itself with civil law, but it should always be a prophetic light to the world.

15

DO THEY ALL HAVE SUPERPOWERS?

Héritier, like most youngsters, loves superheroes. He can tell you about *Star Wars* and lightsabers. He loves Marvel movies. He likes Spiderman. Most of all, he likes the idea of having superpowers.

After he had been enrolled in his local parish school, Héritier's mother showed him around the parish church. It was one of the oldest churches in Australia, densely populated with generations of statues: Jesus with his burning heart; Mary his mother, standing on a snake; St. Joseph with his lily; St. Michael the Archangel about to skewer a dragon; and St. Lucy with her eyeballs in a bowl in her right hand. Héritier is a thoughtful boy. He looked at all the statues. He looked long and hard at St. Michael the Archangel with his wings and his sword. Then he turned to his mother and, with the utmost innocence, asked, "Do they all have superpowers?"

The short answer is yes. The longer answer is that their superpowers are not quite what is portrayed in the statues. The angels and saints don't possess their own superpowers. Rather, they have the power of God's love. This is a supernatural power, even stronger than a superpower!

Making images of saints and angels, particularly before literacy was widespread, was a way of remembering and learning about the heroes and heroines of our faith. Depictions of Jesus and his apostles, made by Christians in the catacombs of Rome two thousand years ago, can still be seen today. Civil societies similarly erect monuments to great leaders in public places, celebrate legends in halls of fame, and create avenues of statues of sporting immortals, even though some of them are already dead.

It is sometimes said that Catholics worship statues. True, we see devout souls today kneeling before statues and praying their hearts out, but essentially, they are asking the saints to intercede for them with Jesus. They are not worshiping a graven image. As James Corkery puts it, "The canonized saints put faces on holiness. They save us from preoccupation with an abstract ideal of holiness...making concrete and visible what an adventure in saintly living is."[1]

Furthermore, there is also an important element of Christian faith—known as "the Communion of Saints"—which demands that we acknowledge not only the formally canonized saints, but also all the holy women and men who have put their faith in Jesus. The Communion of Saints means in practice that we all belong to each other, whether living or dead, and that we are more connected than separated. The Eucharist, our holy communion, is also a communion of saints, uniting us together in Jesus.

Some ancient saints are indeed said to possess legendary powers. St. Denis of Paris, for example, after he had been decapitated by pagan priests, is said to have picked up his head, washed off the blood, and then carried on preaching the gospel. This was said to have happened in the third century in Montmartre, the Mountain of Martyrs, in Paris. It was said that St. Margaret of Antioch, after being swallowed up by a satanic dragon, cut her way out of its belly. St. Joseph of Cupertino, despite his best efforts not to show off, could not stop himself from flying around the church when he was at prayer. All these people actually existed. The stories about them are taken with a grain of salt today, but nonetheless they must have been outstanding in their faith. More recent Catholic practice continues to associate saints with extraordinary happenings, especially with healings that seem beyond the power of medicine, which, after careful scientific examination, are deemed to be miracles.

The Communion of Saints, whether greatly revered or everyday anonymous saints, shows the ultimate superpower, above all other powers, of the love of God made visible in Jesus. As St. Paul put it, "Neither death, nor life, nor angels, nor rulers, nor things present, nor things to come, nor powers, nor height, nor depth, nor anything else in all creation, will be able to separate us from the love of God in Christ Jesus our Lord" (Rom 8:38–39). We all belong in this communion. This is what we mean when we profess in the Creed that we believe in the Communion of Saints. We are saints with supernatural powers too.

~ ◯ ~

A related question here is "Are there really angels?" The Greek word *angelos* means "messenger." In Christian faith, angels are messengers of God, or "spirits in the divine service" (Heb 1:14). According to the Bible, for the most part angels don't have wings or any other superpowers. Rather, they look like ordinary human beings

---

1. James Corkery, "The Communion of Saints," *The Way* 36, no. 4 (1996): 289.

(see Gen 19:1–2; Judg 6:12; Mark 16:5).[2] In the Book of Revelation, we read of war breaking out in heaven, and "Michael and his angels" fighting against "the dragon and his angels," but there is no mention of wings or swords.

This doesn't mean that talk about angels is nonsense. It is always difficult to talk about realities that are at the edge of our ordinary experience of nature. Indeed, in quantum physics there is a parallel to our talk about angels as messengers of God. Physicists talk about what they call "messenger particles"—like gluons and bosons and maybe even gravitons—to explain a subtle connection that gives rise to forces like electromagnetism and gravity, even though the "messenger particles" are neither precisely messengers nor particles! Scientists are speaking figuratively rather than literally. So also do we speak about angels as messengers of God's power. In faith, and in the experience of some of the faithful, it is believed that God has created persons of a spiritual nature. We call them angels. All we can say, speaking figuratively, is that they are messengers of God, expressions of God's love. Like gravitons, which scientists believe must exist, angels may be beyond physical detection. Nonetheless, we may become aware of them through our spiritual senses,[3] for they are spiritual beings present to God, just as we are embodied spiritual beings present to God. The good angels are the guardians of our lives. Like messenger particles, they communicate the force of God's love. That is their superpower.

---

2. Angels are not to be confused with the cherubim and seraphim, who are said to surround the presence of the most holy God, as described in the visions of Ezekiel and Isaiah, and who have many wings.

3. A spiritual sense is a sixth sense, beyond the five physical senses of touch, taste, smell, sight, and hearing. For more on spiritual senses, see John Honner, *Does God Like Being God?*, chap. 8, "So Where Is God?"

16

IF GOD FORGIVES EVERYONE, WHY DOES HELL EXIST?

In 2015, during a parish visit and a meeting with children and young people, a girl scout asked Pope Francis, "If God forgives everyone, why does hell exist?" Francis acknowledged that this was a very good question. God doesn't send people to hell, he explained. Rather, people choose not to go to God and end up in hell: "You go there because you choose to be there. Hell is wanting to be distant from God because I do not want God's love. This is hell."[1] There are some people, he was saying, whom God wants to forgive, and yet who reject God's offer.

While the Church doesn't talk about sin and hell quite as much as it used to, young people may still worry about whether they might go to hell or, more frequently, whether one of their relatives, who perhaps was guilty of some notorious offense, might go to hell. Francis offers them words of comfort. He says that hell is not literally a fiery furnace and a place of punishment, and paradoxically, that sin can bring us closer to God rather than condemning us to hell. This calls for further investigation.

The Bible begins with stories about how the perfect paradise that God created became a place of strife because humans failed to follow directions and offended God, sometimes out of stupidity, sometimes out of malice. The three most frequently used Hebrew words for such misbehavior, which we generally translate as "sin," mean something like failing to do one's duty, or a breach of promise, or a corrupt and crooked action. Some of these sins are committed by individuals, others by the whole community. Some sins are said to lead to death.

---

1. See Thomas Reese, "Pope Francis and Hell," *Sight Magazine*, April 3, 2018, https://www.sightmagazine.com.au/9071 -essay-pope-francis-and-hell.

Jesus declares at the outset of his ministry that he has come to call sinners (see Luke 5:32). He says that he did not come to condemn but to save (see John 3:17; 8:11). He repeatedly asks his listeners to repent of their sins and to believe in God's love (see Mark 1:15). He is accused of being a friend of sinners (see Matt 11:19). One of the most memorable events in the Gospels concerns an unnamed and uninvited woman, a public sinner, who brings an alabaster jar of perfumed ointment into the house of Simon the Pharisee and comes up behind Jesus, weeping, bathing his feet with her tears, drying them with her hair, kissing his feet, and anointing them with the ointment (see Luke 7:37–38). Why did she do this? In being forgiven she had realized what one theologian called "the incomprehensible prodigality of the divine foolishness of love."[2]

Jesus doesn't condemn or belittle people for being sinners. Rather, it's the exact opposite. He tells them that God wants to gather them in, whether they are lost sheep, prodigal sons, greedy tax collectors, or a woman with many husbands. He tells them that they are loved. He attends to them. He heals and makes whole.

In the New Testament, the Greek word most often used for "sin" is *hamartia*. Originally, *hamartia* meant something like "failing to hit the target." For example, when I fire an arrow and it falls short of the target, this is *hamartia*. The arrow has not done what it was intended to do. In this sense, sin is not so much my deliberate offense against God as it is my failure to be as good as I could be, to be the person God intended me to be. There are other Greek words in the New Testament, often translated as *sin*, that have more serious meanings—like fallen, prodigal, wicked, transgressing, violating, or evil. These kinds of sins do serious injury to others, to society, to creation, and to our own self.

Sin is not vanilla mediocrity. Sin hurts a person. When I am lazy or greedy or vain, I hurt myself. When I steal or mock, I hurt others. When I trash creation, I hurt the Creator. When I neglect the poor and the abandoned, I am hurting Jesus's loved ones. As St. Teresa of Avila put it, sin is the saddest thing, because when I sin, I hurt my best friend Jesus.

Francis has done much to move the Church from a preoccupation with sin as a moral fault to an embrace of the sinner as a human person loved by God. He says, "It is difficult for everything to be clear, precise, outlined neatly. Life is complicated; it consists of grace and sin. He who does not sin is not human. We all make mistakes,

---

2. Karl Rahner, "The Prison Pastorate," in *Mission and Grace*, vol. 3 (London: Sheed & Ward, 1966).

and we need to recognize our weakness." For Jesus, he says, "the sinner comes before the sin."[3]

The girl scout was right—God does want to forgive us—but what then of hell?

~ ◯ ~

Do sinners go to hell? Does hell exist? What is hell? Note that the verb *go* suggests that hell is a place, but this may be a figure of speech. The Church, following the Bible, has consistently held that hell "exists," but is equally clear that hell is more a state than a place. The *Catechism* asserts that hell is "a state of definitive self-exclusion from communion with God and the blessed" (§§1035, 1033). As John Paul II explained, "Rather than a place, hell indicates the state of those who freely and definitively separate themselves from God, the source of all life and joy." Furthermore, he warns against "the improper use of biblical images."[4]

The biblical images of hell can be misleading. They are instructive more because of their variety than because of their horror. *Sheol* means something like a realm of shadows, for good and wicked alike, where people end up after they are buried. It is not a place of fire. *Gehenna*, on the other hand, is an actual place, a valley outside of Jerusalem that became a smoldering garbage dump. Figuratively, *Gehenna* signifies being cast out into constant fire and pain. In the Gospels, this is said to be the place where the wicked, if they do not change their ways, will end up. Then there is *Hades*, a place of torment—though not necessarily with fire—from which the wicked cannot escape. There are also images of people being cast into outer darkness, into lakes of fire, and weeping and gnashing their teeth. This variety suggests that talk about hell is not a literal account of a particular place so much as a set of figurative descriptions of what our existence will be like if we choose to turn away from God. God did not make a hell, and hell is not a place.

While in faith we believe there may be a state called hell, we also believe that it is possible that there is nobody in hell. This is for three reasons. First, given "the incomprehensible prodigality of the divine foolishness of love," it follows that God will do everything possible to draw all creation back into the embrace of divine love—this is called a theology of universal salvation, which will be discussed at greater length in the following chapter. Second, if hell entails a "willful turning away from God" and "a state of definitive self-exclusion from communion with God" (*Catechism* §§1033, 1037), then it seems unlikely that any person who encounters God could deliberately

---

3. Pope Francis, address to religious in Rome (January 3, 2014); and homily, Rome (March 29, 2019).
4. Pope John Paul II, General Audience (July 28, 1999).

and definitively turn away from God. And, finally, there are the interesting implications of that curious phrase in the Apostles' Creed about Jesus descending into hell. Joseph Ratzinger, before he became Pope Benedict XVI, suggested that this might mean hell can never be the same again because now love dwells in it.[5]

This does not mean that we can be absolutely sure that there is nobody in hell. Nor can we lead a life of debauchery, cruelty, and irreverence and expect no consequences. One of the hardest things in life is to admit that we have descended into chaos and been a bad person. In the end, though, only stupid, stubborn pride can exclude us from God's love. This is what we mean when, in the Creed, we profess that we believe in the forgiveness of sins.

---

5. See the first edition of Joseph Ratzinger, *Introduction to Christianity* (London: Burns & Oates, 1969), II.4, "Descended into Hell." This seems at odds with the *Catechism of the Catholic Church* (§633), however, which declares that Jesus did not descend into hell to deliver the damned nor to destroy the hell of damnation.

17

WILL MY DOG GO TO HEAVEN?

This is a child's question. It is a great question. It is about unconditional love and eternal hope. The first response, given the importance of attending to the questioner before answering the question, might be, "What's your dog's name?" and "Is she your very best friend?" If I may say so, this question is very real for me too. My dog is a Cocker Spaniel Poodle cross, fifteen years old, deaf and blind, with perhaps only a month or so to live. She has sat beside me at my morning prayer every day since she was a puppy. She's not precisely a "good" dog, but I do love her. Will my dog go to heaven? The short answer is yes your dog will be in heaven and, figuratively speaking, will be waiting for you at the gate.

Words about heaven—the Greek word is *ouranos*—appear hundreds of times in the New Testament, notably in the opening line of the Our Father. In relation to the child asking this question, we might also note that Jesus says that little children have their angels in heaven (see Matt 18:10) and that it is to the little children that the kingdom of heaven belongs (see Matt 19:14). Surely, then, their pets belong there too.

Strictly speaking, *ouranos* simply means "the sky," but in the New Testament it also means what lies beyond the sky, where God dwells along with other heavenly beings. It is a heaven *beyond* the skies. This heaven is physically quite different from earth. While we tend to imagine heaven as a place somewhere up in the sky, we should try to imagine it as a totally different kind of reality, beyond time and space. Eternity is not time that goes on and on, like a clock that never stops. Eternity is a moment when time stands still forever: it cannot be surpassed, it cannot be completely fathomed, and it never ends.

A young person might find all this difficult to believe. We could gently suggest that we humans do not know everything, and in fact, we know very little even about our material universe. We could suggest that it is quite possible there could be levels of reality that we do not know about. We could suggest that our dreams might be foretastes of heaven, because they occur in a kind of space and time, and a kind of physicality, and yet at a totally different level of reality.

There is a relevant story in the Gospels about the Sadducees, who did not believe in resurrection, asking Jesus a tricky question: "If a woman had seven husbands, one after the other, and then went to heaven, who would be her husband in heaven?" Jesus answered them:

> You know neither the scriptures nor the power of God. For in the resurrection they neither marry nor are given in marriage, but are like angels in heaven. And as for the resurrection of the dead, have you not read what was said to you by God, "I am the God of Abraham, the God of Isaac, and the God of Jacob"? He is God not of the dead, but of the living. (Matt 22:29–32)

In other words, Jesus is telling the Sadducees to broaden their imagination. Resurrection life is not more of earthly life, nor is it earthly life without the bad bits. It is not more of what we know. It is being with God.

Jesus promises his followers that where he goes, to be with his Father in heaven, they too will soon follow (see John 13:36).[1] He tells them that there are many rooms waiting for them in the Father's house (see John 14:2) and their names are written in heaven (see Luke 10:20). While the first Christians were clear that heaven was their destiny and a treasure beyond all others, they were far from sure what heaven was like. Heaven would be different. St. Paul described heaven this way:

> What no eye has seen, nor ear heard,
>   nor the human heart conceived,
> what God has prepared for those who love him. (1 Cor 2:9)

Pope John Paul II thus spoke of heaven in personal rather than physical terms. Heaven is "metaphorically speaking...the dwelling-place of God." He continued:

> We know that the "heaven" or "happiness" in which we will find ourselves is neither an abstraction nor a physical place in the clouds, but a living, personal relationship with the Holy Trinity....Today, personalist language

---

1. For more on resurrection, see John Honner, *Did Jesus Have a Girlfriend?*, chaps. 12 and 13: "Was the Tomb Empty?" and "So Where Is Jesus Now?"

is better suited to describing the state of happiness and peace we will enjoy in our definitive communion with God.[2]

Personalist language is about persons as subjects in relationships rather than about human beings as objects in space and time. Heaven is a perfect relationship rather than a perfect location.

But do God's preparations "for those who love him" include dogs? Or even non-Christians? Some have argued, particularly based on some verses in the Book of Revelation, that only a chosen few will get to heaven. This is called a theology of pre-destination. It holds that many will be excluded from heaven. The closing chapters of the Book of Revelation, for example, describe a heaven that excludes "the dogs and sorcerers and fornicators and murderers and idolaters, and everyone who loves and practices falsehood" (Rev 22:15). But surely, we could say, this is figurative language, and, with tongue in cheek, add that any dogs that practice falsehood are at best only metaphorical dogs, not the actual species, because real dogs cannot tell a lie.

There is plenty of evidence in Scripture to support the belief that God ultimately wants to gather all peoples, indeed the whole of creation, into heaven. Just this morning, for example, as I was praying the morning prayer of the Church, I noticed that the Psalm of the day declares that God gives protection to "humans and animals alike" (Ps 36:6) and the canticle of the day proclaims to God that "all your creatures serve you" (Jdt 16:14).

The idea that God wants all to be saved is called a theology of universal salva-tion. Opposed to a theology of predestination, it holds that God has "a plan for the fullness of time, to gather up all things in him [Christ], things in heaven and things on earth" (Eph 1:10). This clearly includes dogs. If God is love, then this love is universal. The *Catechism* quotes St. Thérèse of Lisieux, in full capital letters, "LOVE...INCLUDES ALL OTHERS; IT'S A UNIVERSE OF ITS OWN, COMPRISING ALL TIME AND SPACE—IT'S ETERNAL." Heaven, the Church teaches, is "the profound common destiny of the material world and humanity" where "happiness will fill and surpass all the desires of peace" (§§826, 1028, 1046, 1048). There seems to be plenty of room for dogs.

Love of animals is particularly prominent in St. Francis of Assisi's spirituality, which celebrates God's universal presence in nature. "Francis came to see that *all creatures form one family of creation*."[3] If we are part of one family, then all that God

---

2. Pope John Paul II, General Audience (July 21, 1999).
3. Jack Wintz, *Will I See My Dog in Heaven?* (Brewster, MA: Paraclete Press, 2009), xiii.

loves and all that we love will be gathered in heaven. Another Franciscan, Richard Rohr, thus wrote,

> Love has you. Love *is* you. Love alone, and your deep need for love, recognizes love everywhere else. Remember that you already are what you are seeking....All you have loved in your life and been loved by are eternal and true. That is why it is very good theology to believe that your dogs, cats, and horses will be with you in heaven.[4]

Our dog has an infallibly accurate nose for people who don't like dogs. She would sidle up beside them and rest her head on one of their feet. Some would try to push her away or move their foot. She would then rest her head beside their foot. I suspect she will do this in heaven—metaphorically, if not literally—especially on the feet of those saints who think there should be no dogs in heaven.

A more serious and telling account of heaven comes at the end of Dostoevsky's novel *The Brothers Karamazov*. The three brothers have to deal with much pain and evil in their lives. The youngest, Alyosha Karamazov, tries to escape the horrors of the world by entering a monastery, but there he discovers he is called to love life, to go into the world, and to become a kind of teacher. After a ragged student called Ilyusha dies from tuberculosis, his classmates gather for the funeral. The rebellious Kolya then asks his teacher *the* tricky question:

> "Karamazov," cried Kolya, "can it be true what's taught us in religion, that we shall all rise again from the dead and shall live and see each other again, all, Ilyusha too?"
>
> "Certainly we shall all rise again, certainly we shall see each other and shall tell each other with joy and gladness all that has happened!" Alyosha answered, half laughing, half enthusiastic.
>
> "Ah, how splendid it will be!" broke from Kolya.

Some young people, unlike Kolya, might still be unconvinced. I can only say that, for me, heaven makes sense of our living and loving, which otherwise would be inconsequential and incomplete. As Francis observes, this world foreshadows the

---

4. Richard Rohr, "Love Is Stronger than Death" (CAC podcast, 2017) adapted from Richard Rohr, *Immortal Diamond: The Search for Our True Self* (San Francisco: Jossey-Bass, 2013), 178–79.

fullness of reality, which is God's reality: "Here we are passing through. We are made for heaven, for eternal life, to live forever."[5]

Heaven is our reasonable hope for happiness, and it will be all the happier for having dogs. And non-Catholic Christians. And every other religion. And atheists. Maybe even cats. This is what we mean when, in the Creed, we profess that we believe in the resurrection of the body and life everlasting. Amen.

5. Pope Francis, public audience (May 10, 2020). He might have been echoing St. Mary Mackillop: "Remember we are but travelers here."

Part Two

ADVANCED TOPICS

18

WHY IS TONIGHT DIFFERENT FROM ALL OTHER NIGHTS? A DOMESTIC CHURCH

"Why is tonight different from all other nights?" This is possibly the most frequently asked question in the history of religion. It is the question that the youngest capable child present asks at the beginning of a Jewish family's celebration of the Passover. This day is a feast day and a holiday: a *holy day*. After the selected child asks this question, which is about why they eat certain foods in a certain way, family members explain the meaning behind these rituals and then read the stories and psalms about the Exodus, about how the Lord God has delivered the Israelites out of captivity. Faith begins at home.

Jesus was born in a domestic setting, not in a great church. He learned his faith from his parents, growing in wisdom and knowledge. He was homeschooled. We have learned much about homeschooling during the COVID-19 pandemic. Big church and little church have their place in our lives, but the most important church is home church. Home sustains faith.

A young mother who says a prayer every night with her children—teaching them to thank God for all the good things of the day and to remember the needs of their friends who are sick and suffering—is sowing the seeds of faith. A couple who may have used some sharp words, but then embraces and apologizes and forgives, is celebrating a sacrament. A home that is open to the homeless is welcoming Christ.

The place where we live and love and pray is a home church or, as the Second Vatican Council put it, a "domestic church" (*Lumen Gentium* 11).[1] Pope Francis, writing on *The Joy of Love*, reminds us that the New Testament speaks of "churches that meet in homes" and suggests that "a family's living space could turn into a domestic church, a setting for the Eucharist, the presence of Christ seated at its table." While

---

1. See also Pope John Paul II, *Familiaris Consortio*, The Family in the Modern World (November 22, 1981), no. 21.

focusing on Christian marriage as the "ideal" model of a domestic church, he also notes that some other "forms of union" realize this ideal "in at least a partial and analogous way" (*Amoris Laetitia* 15, 292).

We might all feel a little helpless about the state of the global Church, but that does not preclude each of us from developing our own domestic church, whether we are families, couples, or even, at some stages of life, on our own. A domestic church develops its own special prayers and practices and holy places. Some homes have a small shrine, or an heirloom of religious art. Some have a "Jesus room" for those who have nowhere to lay their head. Many homes have prayers before a meal. A domestic church has its own spiritual music and rituals. It finds its own practical ways to accompany and serve the bereft, the homeless, the sick, and the lonely. We learn gratitude for love and life. We learn to live in God's company.

At an Easter Vigil Mass for children in our parish, our rather progressive parish priest started to engage the children with some questions, as was his usual excellent practice. He promised to give them some Easter eggs, but said he needed to ask a few questions first. What is Easter about? Is it about chocolate? Diana, aged eight at the time and quite interested in chocolate, put up her hand. She spoke quickly and solemnly. "It's to celebrate the death and resurrection of Jesus Christ." Fr. George nearly fell over backward. Diana belongs to an extended family that enjoys preparing meals together, that takes care of strangers, that plays and sings Christmas carols, and has the youngest capable child leading a simple prayer of thanks and grace before dinner. Faith begins at home. Home sustains faith.

POSTSCRIPT: SOME IDEAS FOR CHRISTMAS AND EASTER WITH CHILDREN

There are many opportunities, particularly at Christmas, to explore questions about faith. Why is Christmas important? Why do we have Christmas presents and Christmas trees? Why do we put lights and angels on the trees? What is Kris Kindle?

First, the easy question: Kris Kindle is a deplorable corruption of the beautiful German word *Christkindl*, which means something like "dearest Christ child." Second, Christmas trees come from Protestant Germany, perhaps as a counterpart to the Catholics having a Christmas crib in their homes, because statues were regarded by Protestants as bordering on idolatry. The first decorations on the Christmas tree were brightly wrapped sweets to be given to children. The tree was viewed as a new "tree of life," replacing the one that God had planted in the center of the Garden of Eden. The red baubles on the Christmas tree represented the fruit, supposedly apples, that Adam and Eve ate from a second tree, the "tree of the knowledge of good and evil," in the center of the Garden of Eden. Jesus was seen as the new Adam, and so Christmas was a whole new start for humankind. The candles perhaps represented the stars seen at Jesus's birth. The angels might have been added by Catholics for the same purpose. So powerful was the symbolism of the Christmas tree that it was banned in Communist Russia. Ironically, Communist Russia collapsed on Christmas Day, 1991.

Many families place a Christmas crib under their Christmas tree and then, on Christmas morning, children would find baby Jesus in the cradle in the center of the crib. Statues of the three wise men might appear near the back door of the house and each night, for eleven days, they would be seen to move a few feet closer to the crib. On the morning of the Feast of the Epiphany, the twelfth day of Christmas, they would be found at the crib, giving their presents to Jesus. That is how the practice of giving Christmas presents began. It reflects the gift that Jesus is to the world and the gifts brought by the Magi to Jesus. Christmas crackers contain crowns, originally a reminder of the Magi, sometimes known as the Three Kings from the Orient. In fact, they weren't kings—they were learned scholars, astronomers as well as astrologers. They were the scientists of their time, seeking after a wonder of nature. They found a divine wonder.

That is the gift of Christmas. Stories about St. Nicholas, a real bishop who actually and secretly gave presents to poor children at Christmastime, further encouraged the practice of giving gifts. He became Santa Claus, and the rest is history. Teenagers may not be much interested in all of this. They may prefer to revisit movies like *Polar Express* or *Elf*, which can become an alternative feel-good ritual, if rather ambiguous and shallow. However, if you were to invite a group of talented young people to busk outside department stores at Christmas—especially stores that have canceled the word Christmas—to sing carols and wish everyone a happy Christmas, you might just get a response.

Easter is another highpoint in the life of a domestic Church, especially when there are children present. Yet questions like "Why do we have Easter eggs?" and "Why are Easter eggs hollow?" are possibly the least asked questions on the day. But Easter, like Passover, is a holy day. It tells the story of an empty tomb and life beyond death. It celebrates Jesus being alive with us, a triumph of hope over disappointment. We celebrate Easter with eggs because eggs symbolize new life, and the Easter egg is empty because the tomb was empty.

In a Greek Orthodox family, it is common to play a game with Easter eggs that goes like this. One person says "*Christos anesti*—Christ has risen." A second then says "*Alithos anesti*—Truly He is risen." The second person then gently taps their egg into the first speaker's egg until one egg cracks. The winner, with the unbroken egg, then says "*Christos anesti*—Christ has risen" and waits for someone new to reply "*Alithos anesti*—Truly He is risen." And so, the game continues until there is only one unbroken egg left. The winner is then promised special blessings and privileges throughout the year. *Alithos anesti.*

19

CATHEDRALS AND CARAVANS: A SYNODAL CHURCH

O ne of the most significant changes in the Church in the past few years has been Pope Francis's insistence on synodality. Being synodal means traveling together. A synodal Church is not a new idea so much as a return to the freshness of the beginning of the Church, a gathering of all the believers guided by the Holy Spirit.

The word *sunodia*—or synod—comes from two Greek words that literally mean "together on the way." It occurs only once in the New Testament, but it occurs at the heart of a dramatic event when Jesus was twelve years old and went missing in Jerusalem. His parents had assumed he was somewhere among the group of travelers who were returning to Nazareth. The Gospel describes them as a *sunodia*, which is often translated into English as a "caravan" (see Luke 2:44). In this case, however, Jesus was not on the road. He was in the temple. The *sunodia* was incomplete without him.

Jesus's ministry was largely spent on the road. Occasionally, though, he sat down by a well, or in a boat, or on a hill, or near the temple. Sometimes, he sat down to teach; other times he sat to rest and to contemplate what was happening around him. Often, he taught in synagogues,[1] and occasionally he visited the temple. Synodality involves a journey, but it also entails contemplating what is happening around us, and sometimes sitting and listening to what others have to say.

The equivalent of the temple today, for Catholics, is the cathedral. A cathedral is the opposite of a synod in that it is relatively immoveable and unchanging. A cathedral is a church in which the seat of the bishop is placed, usually on the sanctuary. That's what the original Greek word, *kathedra*, meant, a place where you sat down.

---

1. The word *synagogue* has similar origins to the word *synodality*. It comes from two Greek words that mean "to bring together."

Cathedrals are the locus of teaching and ritual in the life of the Church. The authority of the bishop comes from the Holy Spirit and guides the people.

The Catholic Church is diverse rather than uniform. There are times when some elements threaten division, but the Church must transcend division and seek unity. This requires listening. This is how the cathedral and the caravan go together. Synodality offers an attractive image of the way a Christ-centered Church would proceed. In this image, the Church is a caravan of solidarity, guided by Jesus Christ, and so having direction and intentionality. It is Christ's Way. Occasionally the Church stops for a rest and a cathedral is built.

The word *synod* was commonly used in the early Church to describe local gatherings of bishops and priests. In 1965, following the reforms of the Second Vatican Council, Paul VI established the Synod of Bishops as a permanent institution to assist in the governance of the Church. Fifty years later, Francis insisted on including the laity and emphasized the preeminence of the Holy Spirit:

> A synodal Church is a Church which listens, which realizes that listening "is more than simply hearing." It is a mutual listening in which everyone has something to learn. The faithful people, the college of bishops, the Bishop of Rome: all listening to each other, and all listening to the Holy Spirit, the "Spirit of truth," in order to know what He "says to the Churches."[2]

Francis uses the word *synodal* not just to describe a structure but, more importantly, to shape an attitude, a readiness to listen, a way of inhabiting a structure. Synodality reminds us that how we inhabit an organizational structure is more important than the structure itself. Being synodal means being inclusive of and listening to everybody. Synodality is not, however, the same as democracy, because the minority voice might be the voice of the Holy Spirit. Nor does synodality mean making compromises, which is the least satisfactory way of resolving diverse views. Rather, it may mean embracing several views, within agreed boundaries. It may require everyone to leave their boats behind, striving to come to a new place together, and developing a closer and more loving unity. Thus, in launching the process for the 2022 Synod of Bishops, Francis notes that synodality

---

2. Pope Francis, Address at the celebration of the 50th Anniversary of the institution of the Synod of Bishops (October 17, 2015). Some of this chapter draws on my work as a member of a writing group preparing for the 2021 Plenary Council of the Catholic Church in Australia. See https://plenarycouncil.catholic.org.au/wp-content/uploads/2020/05/PC2020-thematic-papers-2.pdf. Used with permission.

offers us the opportunity to become a Church of closeness. Let us keep going back to God's own "style," which is closeness, compassion and tender love. God has always operated that way. If we do not become this Church of closeness with attitudes of compassion and tender love, we will not be the Lord's Church....The Holy Spirit guides us where God wants us to be, not to where our own ideas and personal tastes would lead us.[3]

Being part of a caravan goes back to the beginnings of the stories about our faith, when God tells Abraham, "Go from your country and your kindred and your father's house to the land that I will show you" (Gen 12:1). Thus it is that the oldest texts in the Bible remember Abraham as "a wandering Aramean" (Deut 26:5). Today, in the same spirit, Francis challenges us to leave "our personal tastes" behind and to travel into a new country. The way is known, it is synodal. The destination is yet to be revealed.

Being a synod is different from having a method. Method means following specific rules to achieve a predetermined goal. In a method, it is important to follow the recipe exactly. A synodal Church, however, is less concerned about predetermined goals. It is not disorganized, but it makes room for the Spirit. It attends to prophets and stragglers. It is inclusive of persons rather more than being inclusive of ideologies. As well as acknowledging the authority of the cathedral, it appreciates that every person is a doorway into the mystery that is the Body of Christ. As French theology professor Agnès Desmazières notes, "Synodality means taking the risk of surprise."[4]

---

3. Pope Francis, Address for the Opening of the Synod (October 9, 2021).

4. Céline Hoyeau, "Synodality Means Taking the Risk of Surprise," *La Croix International* (January 3, 2022), https://international.la-croix.com/news/religion/synodality-means-taking-the-risk-of-surprise/15421.

20

MARIAN AND PETRINE: A HOLY AND APOSTOLIC CHURCH

There is such a thing as everyday holiness. Holiness is more than piety. Holy people are everywhere. They are joyful, happy, humble, caring, bold, prayerful, patient, persevering, passionate, peacemaking, healing, and making whole. Holy people are comfortable whether alone or in company. They do not seek limelight. They see the glory of life. They are other-centered. Each is holy in their own unique way. This is what closeness to God looks like in practice.[1]

This book has been more about information than about holiness. It has been more concerned with answering questions about the Church than about the holiness of the members of the Church. Information alone, however, does not change hearts. We need a Church that *lives* the faith as well as, and more than, a Church that *teaches* the faith. All members of the Church should give priority to holiness. The Church is only authentic when it is holy.

John Paul II understood this. Reflecting on the role of Mary, the Mother of Jesus, in the Church (the Marian dimension of the Church) and that of Peter (the Petrine dimension of the Church), he gave primacy to the holiness of Mary:

Although the Church possesses a "hierarchical" structure, nevertheless this structure is totally ordered to the holiness of Christ's members....The Second Vatican Council, confirming the teaching of the whole of tradition, recalled that in the hierarchy of holiness it is *precisely the "woman,"* Mary of Nazareth, who is the "figure" of the Church. She "precedes" everyone on the path to holiness....In this sense, one can say that the Church is *both* "Marian" and "Apostolic-Petrine." (*Mulieris Dignitatis* 27)

---

1. These are some of the themes Francis explores in his exhortation on the Call to Holiness, *Gaudete et Exsultate* (2018).

In an address to the bishops and cardinals of the Vatican, John Paul II made the same point with greater emphasis, as if cautioning the hierarchy about overreaching its power:

> The Church too, like Mary, lives in grace, in submission to the Holy Spirit, interprets the signs and needs of the times in his light, and advances along the path of faith in full docility to the voice of the Spirit....This *Marian* profile is just as—if not more so—fundamental and characterizing for the Church as the *apostolic and Petrine* profile, to which it is profoundly united. Also, in this aspect of the Church, Mary precedes the pilgrim People of God....The Marian dimension of the Church precedes the Petrine one, even though it is closely united and complementary to it.[2]

This teaching became enshrined in the *Catechism*: "The 'Marian' dimension of the Church precedes the 'Petrine'" (§773).

The Marian dimension of the Church reflects the life of Mary, radically open to the Holy Spirit, a model of holiness. The opening chapter of the Acts of the Apostles describes the beginnings of the Church when, following Jesus's resurrection and ascension, the apostles gathered in the upper room in Jerusalem "constantly devoting themselves to prayer, together with certain women, including Mary the mother of Jesus, as well as his brothers" (Acts 1:13–14). These verses capture the Marian dimension of the Church: it is feminine, prayerful, serving, familial, bound by love to Jesus, inclusive, lay, faithful, and holy.[3] The Marian dimension is the heart of the Church, attuned to Jesus, and guided by the Holy Spirit. It is the underlying inspiration of the Church. This is Mary, "preceding the pilgrim People of God."

The Petrine dimension of the Church is characterized by the ministry of Peter—along with the apostles—as leader, pastor, and teacher. It finds its expression in the ministries of the pontiff, bishops, and priests. The Petrine dimension has become masculine, celibate, orderly, hierarchical, and exclusive.

Giving priority to the Marian dimension of the Church does not mean doing away with the Petrine dimension. Each informs the other. Giving priority to the Marian dimension of the Church does not mean disregarding or disrespecting bishops. They may be as holy, if not more holy, than most of us. The exercise of their office,

---

2. Pope John Paul II, Address to the Roman Curia (Christmas, 1988).

3. Pope John Paul II's thinking on the Marian dimension of the Church was influenced by the theologian Hans Urs von Balthasar, for whom "the radiant heart of the Church is lay, faithful, and holy." See John McDade, "Von Balthasar and the Office of Peter in the Church," *The Way* 44, no. 4 (2005): 101.

however, as for most leaders, can demand attending to governance, making difficult decisions, applying rules and regulations, and having long work hours. The burdens of office can isolate bishops from the people.

Francis is aware of this conundrum. At a gathering of Italian bishops, his closing words not only recognized Mary at the heart of the Church, but also described the practical implications of being a tender and compassionate Church on pilgrimage: "Being pastors also means to be ready to walk in the midst of and behind the flock: capable of listening to the silent story of the suffering and bearing up the steps of those who are afraid of not succeeding; careful to raise up, to reassure, and inspire hope."[4] His program for the renewal of the Church calls for a greater emphasis on the Marian dimension of the Church. Canadian theologian Josephine Lombardi thus writes,

> Pope Francis' vision for the Church includes the plan to "mercify" the world, to heal our image of God, a plan that has a therapeutic or Marian dimension that accompanies the juridical or Petrine dimension. This rediscovery of mercy is rooted in a rediscovery or recovery of the Marian dimension, an approach that reads vulnerability in people, assesses and addresses human need....The Marian tells the Petrine why people act the way they do, diagnoses them and leads them to Jesus for healing....This appears to be the vision of Pope Francis: his "program of life." The ocean of God's mercy is wide.[5]

Healing is about making whole. Holiness is about being whole. A Church that is holy will be a welcoming and healing Church, a uniting Church, a whole Church. The Marian dimensions of unity, holiness, and inclusion take precedence. This is why, in the Creed, we profess that we believe in a one, holy, catholic, and apostolic church. The ordering of the words is significant.

---

4. Pope Francis, Address to the Italian Bishops (May 23, 2013).
5. Josephine Lombardi, "Mercy and Beyond: Pope Francis' Marian 'Program of Life,'" *Ecce Mater Tua* 2 (2019): 24.

CONCLUSION

Where to from here? A Church for the Future

My answers to Junior's question from chapter 1—"Church? What's that all about?"—have for the most part rested on a three-line refrain:

> the Church is about the important things in life;
>
> the Church is about all the baptized, in their great variety, on a journey together;
>
> and the Church is more about faith and following the way of Jesus than it is about religion and conforming to moralisms and rules.

This refrain calls for two further considerations. First, because it exists in history, the Church remains a religion, a human organization, with its authorities and rules and factions and crises. Second, because it is a continuation of God's mission, it also exists in the sacramental context of eternal self-giving love, with its holiness and mysticism and hope.

The questions that I hear many adult Christians ask about the Church verge on the pessimistic: "Can the Church ever change?" and "What hope have we got?" Some are more optimistic, like "What will the Church of the future look like?" Young people believe that the Church can change, and they are right. History shows that the Church can change,[1] and since the first preaching of the Gospel, Christians have been called to change their ways and draw closer to Jesus. The call to repent and believe applies to all followers of Jesus, not just to egregious sinners. It applies to me, to you,

---

1. See John Honner, *Does God Like Being God?*, chap. 4: "Can Expressions of Faith Change?"

and to the whole Church. The Church is constantly being called to change—not at a superficial level but deep in its heart.

But what hope do we have? Young people are our hope. And they have a vision for the future: "Today's young people are longing for an authentic Church. We want to say, especially to the hierarchy of the Church, that they should be a transparent, welcoming, honest, inviting, communicative, accessible, joyful and interactive community."[2]

The key for the future of the Church, as it was for Abraham when he started the wandering journey of faith more than three thousand years ago, is not *where it is heading* but *how it is traveling*. Is it traveling in the way of Jesus, guided by the Holy Spirit? Is it holy? Does it show the face of God? Is it caring for the poor, the sick, and the outcast? Is it seeking unity? Is it welcoming? Is it listening? Is it a Church that is responding to the needs of the world?

Jesus tells us to leave everything and to follow him. That's when, like the rich young man, we learn that the caravan of faith has its costs. The Christian community may not be a glorious Church full of sinless women and men. There will be wounds. Jesus said his burden was light but, as the Lutheran theologian Dietrich Bonhoeffer put it, there is a cost to discipleship. The way we carry the burden counts. If we are going to follow Jesus and take up the burdens of faith, we might need to take lessons from the community of saints in learning to walk with a lightness of step,[3] perhaps light enough to even walk on water.

The real challenge is not so much knowing about the Church as being Church. It is one thing to know about Christian life and another thing to live a Christian life. We are called to be authentic in our Christian living, to find God in all things, to be self-giving in love, to be free in the Spirit of Jesus, to embrace our burdens, to be courageous, and to be joyful. We might then look like a Church that means what it says, an authentic Church, a Church with the freshness of the beginning.

---

2. Synod on Young People, *Instrumentum Laboris: Working Document* (2018), no. 67. See nos. 67–69.
3. See Mary Oliver's poem "Heavy" in her collection of poems *Thirst* (Boston: Beacon Press, 2006), 53–54.